EXCELLENCE
IN
LEADERSHIP

Books by John White, published by IVP

The Cost of Commitment
Eros Defiled
The Fight
Healing the Wounded (with Ken Blue)
The Masks of Melancholy
Parents in Pain
People in Prayer
The Race

John White

EXCELLENCE IN LEADERSHIP

The pattern of Nehemiah

Inter-Varsity Press

INTER-VARSITY PRESS
38 De Montfort Street, Leicester LE1 7GP, England

First British edition 1986

British Library Cataloguing in Publication Data

White, John, *1924 Mar. 5 –*
   Excellence in leadership: the pattern of
Nehemiah.
   1. Christian leadership
   I. Title
   248.4   BV652.1

ISBN 0-85110-482-7

Printed in Great Britain by Cox & Wyman Ltd, Cardiff Road, Reading

Inter-Varsity Press is the publishing division of the Universities and Colleges Christian Fellowship (formerly the Inter-Varsity Fellowship), a student movement linking Christian Unions in universities and colleges throughout the United Kingdom and the Republic of Ireland, and a member movement of the International Fellowship of Evangelical Students. For information about local and national activities write to UCCF, 38 De Montfort Street, Leicester LE1 7GP.

1

Meeting
the Man

The details of my first meeting with him are hazy in my mind. God sent him to me during my early university years to help me overcome some formidable challenges. He has been a close companion ever since. I cannot overstate my gratitude for all he has taught me. Though we were separated by more than two millennia and could meet only as he stepped repeatedly from the black print of my Bible, Nehemiah was as real to me as my twentieth-century brothers and sisters.

A Friend in Need

Nehemiah put his very being into his journal, which is incorporated into the book we now call by his name. As I read I can feel his heartbeats, sense the trembling of his fingers, know the heaviness of his groans, see the quickening of his triumphs. What wisdom he had! And how he drummed the basic lessons of leadership into me! I have forgotten none of them and have gone back to him time and again for reassurance.

As a medical student I had a special need of him. He was a leader. And so, whether I wanted to be or not, was I. To be sure, I had enough

ambition to lead, but ambition alone is worse than useless. I was hopelessly naive and soon out of my depth. I was also frightened. Responsibilities and pressures that far exceeded my natural capacities increased
as I became, in a relatively short time, the national student chairman of
British Inter-Varsity.

But I was motivated by more than ambition. God had given me a
genuine hunger for his glory among and a true pastoral concern for
British university students. I led them because I wanted to serve them.
I was destined to be girded with a towel and to wash feet—and I knew
it. By night I anxiously walked the streets of my native city Manchester,
praying for British students with my rain-washed face to the skies. I cried
out to God as Lancashire drizzle trickled coldly down the back of my
neck. During this period Nehemiah comforted and instructed me. As I
gained experience by putting lessons learned from him into practice,
so in time I began to instruct others.

I continued to do so as I shifted my work to Latin America. As my
responsibilities increased there, I chose to expound the book of Nehemiah at the first Latin American leadership conference in Cochabamba,
Bolivia. That conference saw the birth of the Latin American Fellowship
of Evangelical Students. A small international team served the infant
body. Samuel Escobar and René Padilla were there along with two
pioneers, Bob Young and Ruth Siemens. I acted as coordinator of the
team. And Nehemiah became a sort of patron saint of the new movement—or at least a guiding light to young student leaders facing the
awesome task of evangelizing a continent. Eventually Samuel Escobar
incorporated the addresses I had given and some articles I had written
into a book published in Spanish by Ediciones Certeza.

Years passed. As one responsibility replaced another, I continued to
be fascinated and instructed by the life and words of this man of action.
And as I grew older I gleaned more from him. It was the man, not the
book, that held me. I introduced him to a church I pastored, presented
him a second time to Latin American student leaders and recently talked
about him at a series of conferences in Australia. Always it is the com-
pelling individuality of this unique character that holds, guides and

inspires me. He has become my model for leadership.

Cupbearer to the King

Like millions of Jews throughout history, Nehemiah knew the problems of being in a minority. And like many Jews, he knew what it was to be successful. He had risen to a prominent position, that of cupbearer to the Persian emperor Artaxerxes I, the most powerful ruler of that day. As cupbearer it was his duty to taste the wine from the king's cup before handing the cup personally to the king, a sort of personal guarantee that the wine was not poisoned.

He was what we might call a top security agent. We may be sure that since the safety of a powerful ruler as well as the stability of the Persian Empire were at stake, his appointment would not be made lightly. It would be most unlikely, for example, that influential friends could have gotten him the post. Rather he would be chosen for well-tried personal qualities like a stable character, sharp eyes, sharp wits, common sense, initiative and a grasp of palace intrigue. And since his own life might depend on the way he carried out his job, we could add the quality of attention to detail. All of these become evident as a picture of him emerges from the autobiography we find in our Bibles.

No doubt Nehemiah would want to know all about the wine before it was poured. He would supervise every stage of its purchase and storage as well as its pouring. Members of the palace ménage would be obliged to respond to his authority. He would be an influential, if not a powerful, figure around the palace. One cupbearer referred to in the book of Tobit appears to have been a prime minister.

Nehemiah had other qualities that were not only important in his job as cupbearer, but necessary for the life work that lay ahead of him, a life work for which his palace duties represented the final phase of his preparation. He would ultimately be given the task of revitalizing the sacked city of Jerusalem by rebuilding its walls.

The chapters that follow are really a series of essays about him, not an exposition of the book that bears his name (though each chapter will necessarily incorporate exposition). Each essay is based on a passage in Nehemiah—usually one of the chapters that are taken from his personal memoirs. Inevitably there will be repetition, for certian themes recur like leitmotifs as his character develops.

I have included the relevant Scripture passages, sometimes long ones, at the beginning of each chapter. After reading them, you may also want to glance back at them from time to time as you move through the rest of the text. Sometimes I have referred to every verse in the Scripture passage. And even when I fail to do so (for instance, in the somewhat repetitive passage about who worked next to whom on the wall), there are intriguing insights in the Scripture text that I would not want you to miss. With one exception (Neh 8:1—9:5 discussed in chapter eight) the Scripture passages are drawn from Nehemiah's personal records and are those best suited to illustrate his character.

Not all of the book of Nehemiah was written by him. What we now call the book of Nehemiah was probably part of a longer work, namely, Ezra-Nehemiah. The first seven chapters of the book of Nehemiah are written by Nehemiah using the first person singular. The chapters that follow are written in the third peson, presumably by the compiler of Ezra-Nehemiah (possibly Ezra himself) who had made use of the material Nehemiah wrote. The book concludes with a further lengthy passage (13:4-31) written by Nehemiah himself about his second period as governor. (See Derek Kidner's discussion in his commentary *Ezra & Nehemiah*, pp. 136-39.)

The setting of the book of Nehemiah is the rebuilding of a nation. Almost a hundred and fifty years before (587 B.C.) the Babylonians had sacked Jerusalem and the southern kingdom of Judah and exiled its citizens. But after Babylon fell to the Persians, King Cyrus reversed Babylonian policy and allowed some Jewish groups to return to Jerusalem in 538 B.C. Their first acts were to build an altar and rebuild the Temple. (These events are described in the first six chapters of the book of Ezra.) Their next concern was to make the city defensible again. And in 445 B.C. Nehemiah comes to Jerusalem to complete this very task, to build the city walls.

Thus the book of Nehemiah serves primarily to unfold for us part of

God's ongoing plan for his people. But always it is the man, his character and his leadership that hold my interest. I present these reflections with the hope that they will help Christians young or old who face leadership responsibilities. I pray that as I draw back the curtain you will be able to watch Nehemiah re-enact his life on stage and that seeing him you will be gripped as fiercely and changed as radically as I have been.

For Individuals or Groups

1. Describe one or two leaders that you admire. What qualities stand out in your mind? Why?
2. How would you define leadership?
3. What kinds of leadership experiences have you had?
4. What positive results have you seen from your work?
5. What problems or difficulties have you faced?
6. What do you especially want to learn through this study of Nehemiah?

2

The Leader & Prayer

1 *THE WORDS OF NEHEMIAH SON OF HACALIAH:*
In the month of Kislev in the twentieth year, while I was in the citadel of Susa, ²*Hanani, one of my brothers, came from Judah with some other men, and I questioned them about the Jewish remnant that survived the exile, and also about Jerusalem.*

³*They said to me, "Those who survived the exile and are back in the province are in great trouble and disgrace. The wall of Jerusalem is broken down, and its gates have been burned with fire."*

⁴*When I heard these things, I sat down and wept. For some days I mourned and fasted and prayed before the God of heaven.* ⁵*Then I said:*

"O LORD, God of heaven, the great and awesome God, who keeps his covenant of love with those who love him and obey his commands, ⁶*let your ear be attentive and your eyes open to hear the prayer your servant is praying before you day and night for your servants, the people of Israel. I confess the sins we Israelites, including myself and my father's house, have committed against you.* ⁷*We have acted very wickedly toward you. We have not obeyed the commands, decrees and laws you gave your servant Moses.*

⁸*"Remember the instruction you gave your servant Moses, saying, 'If you are unfaithful, I will scatter you among the nations,* ⁹*but if*

*you return to me and obey my commands, then even if your exiled
people are at the farthest horizon, I will gather them from there and
bring them to the place I have chosen as a dwelling for my Name.'*

*[10]"They are your servants and your people, whom you redeemed
by your great strength and your mighty hand. [11]O Lord, let your ear
be attentive to the prayer of this your servant and to the prayer of
your servants who delight in revering your name. Give your servant
success today by granting him favor in the presence of this man."*
I was cupbearer to the king.

Then our story opens, Nehemiah is a leader-in-training. He
doesn't know, however, that he is about to face his final test.
His lifelong training is about to end.

Put another way, he is like an embryonic butterfly, shaped to perfection in a cocoon, without every having tried his wings. His cocoon is
the summer palace at Susa, the capital of the Persian Empire. His graduating examination was to be an ordeal from which he would emerge
from the cocoon trembling, wings, as it were, still wet, teetering on
newly released legs before taking flight.

We see Nehemiah's reactions to the ordeal as we read his prayer that
opens the book. Nine of his prayers are recorded in the book of Nehemiah. Most of them are brief, spur-of-the-moment prayers. The one we
shall examine in this chapter is more substantial and affords us deep
insight into his character. It is one of the classic prayers of Scripture.

Yet when the test begins, he is only aware that he faces an appalling
question, a question that demands he put his own life on the line in
a more perilous sense than when he hands the wine daily to the king.

But if Nehemiah's prayer was important to Nehemiah, it is also important to us. A friend of mine once said, "I learned to pray by being
invited to join with certain old prayer warriors. To hear them pray was
an education." We cannot pray with Nehemiah. What we can do is
overhear him as he prays, trying to discover the secrets of his historic
pleading.

Let us then examine the circumstances surrounding the prayer, as well as its contents. In doing so, we shall learn much about prayer and how God used Nehemiah's active prayer life to mold him into a godly leader. Perhaps we will also perceive the terrifying nature of Nehemiah's "graduation examination."

Body Blow

The book opens as Hanani, a kinsman (possibly a brother) of Nehemiah, comes from distant Jerusalem along with some friends to see him (Neh 1:2). They bring news of destroyed walls, burned gates and the distress and shame of Jerusalem's inhabitants. The news hits Nehemiah like a body blow so that for a prolonged period he weeps, mourns, fasts and prays (1:4).

One hundred forty-one years have passed since the final sack of Jerusalem by Babylonian armies. Unable or unwilling to repent of their idolatry, materialism and covenant breaking, unimpressed by the terrible fate that had befallen the ten northern tribes, scornful of Jeremiah's prophetic messages, the Jews had finally paid a terrible price. Their city was destroyed, their king bereaved, blinded and imprisoned, and they themselves dragged north in chains to be captives and aliens in a foreign land. Nehemiah was a descendant of these captive Jews.

Like all his people Nehemiah looked to Jerusalem as his heart's true home and the center round which his life revolved. Like all Jews he would be stirred by stories of the early waves of settlers as some captives, under more enlightened administrators, were encouraged to return (2 Chron 36:22-23). Seventy years after the sack of Jerusalem, in fulfillment of Jeremiah's prophecy, the Temple was rebuilt (Ezra 6:15-18). Later, word would come of the restoration of the walls. Nehemiah may have been a boy when that news reached Susa.

But temples are not city walls. It would be one thing for the Jews to worship the God of their fathers and quite another for them to make a once rebellious city defensible again. Jerusalem's enemies would see this and, as was their custom, write hostile letters to the capital. We do not know whether their most recent attack on Jerusalem had been carried out with or without the knowledge of the central government in Susa, but most probably they had Susa's support. What we do know is that the labor of months was undone in a few days of fire. The hopes of the Jerusalem Jews for the restoration of their national capital were destroyed. It was this news that so deeply affected Nehemiah.

Emotion and Prayer

Nehemiah went to pray in a storm of emotion. He wept, mourned, fasted. This immediately raises several questions. Is this a model for Christians today? Is weeping prayer more effective, more desirable? Or do we say that weeping, mourning and fasting were cultural characteristics of ancient Jews—or perhaps that Nehemiah personally was an emotional character?

Certainly it is easier to pray when you feel strongly about something. Praying when you are dry is a drag. But I can't say it has no merit, or that God will not respond to it. I used to be a prayer partner of Mrs. Frazier, the widow of the late J. O. Frazier (the great prayer warrior of *Behind the Ranges*). I remember asking her what she did when she felt too dry to pray. "I pray just the same," she said. "Those are the times I most need to pray."

She was right. We must never stop praying because storms of holy ardor no longer sweep across our souls. Of what value is it then to know that Nehemiah was driven to prolonged prayer by profound emotions? Can that knowledge help us when we pray? I believe it can. In our modern preoccupation with facts rather than feelings, we may have forgotten that feelings can sometimes be the thermometers of our spirits. It is as wrong to pay them too little heed as it is to pay them too much.

People pray when they are concerned. If you don't give a hang about something, then you probably won't pray about it. Concern grips us when the Holy Spirit shows us reality—the reality of people's needs and the reality of unseen powers. Switch on the light in a dark room and your feelings will promptly react to what the light reveals—a blood-stained corpse or the organizers of a surprise party. So dryness may mean we are out of touch with reality, that we don't really "see."

I was privileged recently to be at a conference for Christian leaders where there was an opportunity for pastors to go forward if they wanted to repent. Without any manipulation scores responded. Most fell on their knees and many began to sob, some weeping piteously and brokenly. The Holy Spirit had made their sin real to them. Perhaps for the first time they saw it as God saw it. *They were responding to reality,* the reality of the horror of sin.

Years ago in a daily prayer meeting missionary prayer-letter files were passed around. One morning my file contained a letter from a missionary in the Philippines. In it she described her hospitalization in Manila for spinal tuberculosis. Her condition was serious and at that time called for a prolonged period in a sanatorium in a body cast. Unexpectedly (for the woman was a stranger to me) I was not only profoundly shaken but found myself virtually insisting that God heal her right away.

My prayer was remarkable in that I did not believe such healing was possible, and so I was astounded both by the content and the urgency of my own prayer. I suppose you could say that the Holy Spirit was allowing me to "see" two realities—the need of the young missionary, and God's power to do something my theology and medical experience told me was impossible. To the astonishment of her physician, this woman in the Philippines was miraculously healed that same day and soon after became my wife.

The Holy Spirit's illumination will vary in its intensity and degree. At times we will not feel it at all. But it must always be sought. And it will operate not by a direct operation on our feelings so much as by the illumination of our inner vision to reality. God opened Nehemiah's heart to the tragedy of his people, a tragedy that magnified the dishonor to God's name. God enabled him so that he might share God's concern and be caught up into his purposes. This is what God wants for all of us. Of course our absence of feeling can mean we no longer care about the things of God. We have grown lukewarm—a temperature God detests. In that case we are called on to confess our sin and to repent of our lack of devotion to his person. He will meet us, cleanse us and renew us when we do.

What then are we to do when we know we must pray but are void of feeling? We must bring our emptiness to God and inquire about its cause. We must ask the Holy Spirit to open our eyes to realities we have become dulled to. And if we still remain as cold as frozen fish, we must pray anyway, defying the dark powers by exercising our wills to faith and obedience.

God-Centered Faith

We cannot, however, pray without faith, faith both that God exists and that it pays to seek him. Where did Nehemiah's faith spring from?

Faith is not a feeling. It is not even the feeling that something is going to happen in answer to our prayers. Faith may be easier to exercise when such feelings are present. Nevertheless, feelings of that sort never constitute faith. Faith is a response on our part, the obedient response of our wills to who God is and what he says. So notice how Nehemiah's prayer starts: "O LORD, God of heaven, the great and awesome God, who keeps his covenant . . ." (Neh 1:5). His focus reveals the secret of his faith.

You can only have faith in someone to the degree that you know them. In particular you must know two things about them: that they are *able* and that they are *willing* to do what you want them to do. I felt terribly worried about an operation my wife was once to have. Whom could I trust to do it? Then I remembered the "chief." When I was a student, I had assisted him. I had watched his deft gloved hand flawlessly perform the most intricate operations. He never seemed ruffled or upset, however great the crisis. Moreover, he was kind. At once I knew whom I could trust. He could and he would.

These are the two attributes that Nehemiah saw in God. "The great and awesome God" *can* do everything. The God who "keeps his covenant of love" *will* do anything. Nehemiah doubted neither his power nor his kindness. His God could. And his God would.

I have little problem believing in God's power for I have seen too many evidences of it. But I do sometimes doubt his willingness to act on my account. "Who am I," I constantly ask myself, "that he should take any notice of me?" I am learning about his faithfulness and loving-kindness. My God can. And my God will.

But if Nehemiah's faith was based on his knowledge of what God is like, it was made perfect by his knowledge of what God had promised. He quoted what God had said, "Remember the instruction you gave your servant Moses . . ." (Neh 1:8). The promise clinched his faith.

In *Pilgrim's Progress* Christian and Hopeful were caught by Giant Despair and flung into his dungeons in Doubting Castle. Their spirits were low. One early edition describes how Christian suddenly remembered a key named "promises" that was in his bosom. Pulling it out, he found it opened every door leading them out of Doubting Castle. Giant Despair died of apoplexy as he saw the pilgrims escaping. Nehemiah knew how to use the key of promises to escape from his doubts.

Two further points arise out of verse 5. Books about prayer differ about how prayer should begin. Many of them describe different varieties of prayer: prayers of worship, of confession, of supplication and so on. Some of them recommend we start with confession and others that we open with worship. Nehemiah opens with neither. However, he does begin by fixing his eyes on the God he is approaching. And it is by calling God to mind that his faith is kindled and his heart made bold.

Neither confession nor worship, nor any other form of prayer is of itself an ideal way to begin prayer. Rather we prepare our hearts for prayer by fixing our eyes on the person we address. A vision of God will make us ready for whatever form of prayer the Holy Spirit wishes to guide us in, whether it should be confession, intercession, adoration or supplication. Nehemiah's opening sentence tells us who or what filled his horizon, which is what most matters when we pray.

The second issue concerns our obedience. Nehemiah's God preserves his covenant for "those who love him and obey his commands" (Neh 1:5). It is precisely here that our doubts arise about God's willingness to hear us. We fear, and with good reason, that, considering the sin in our hearts, God will not hear us. At this point the matter of confession arises.

Doubtless Nehemiah is conscious of the solemnity of the blessings pronounced on his nation centuries before from Mount Gerizim and the curses from Mount Ebal (Deut 27:11—30:20)—blessings when the covenant was kept and curses when it was violated. His God preserves "his covenant of love with those who love him and obey his commands" (Neh 1:5).

People who love God do what he says. Jesus himself makes the principle clear (Jn 14:21). And the covenant-keeping God has sworn he will never forsake a covenant-keeping people. He and they are bound together by a common purpose and a common life.

But Nehemiah is also conscious that the covenant has been flagrantly violated. The nation's godliness had deteriorated over the centuries. With few exceptions Judah's kings had either tolerated or else actively promoted idolatrous worship. They had formed forbidden alliances with other nations, had ignored social injustices specifically prohibited by the Mosaic law and had persecuted faithful prophets while rewarding prophets who merely flattered them. And most of the people had gone along with their rulers. It was as a result of such persistent and rebellious sin that God had decreed their present captivity.

Nehemiah cannot think of God without remembering this. He is praying "on behalf of his people" and therefore is unable to ignore his people's sin. We would classify this part of his prayer not only as confession but as intercessory, as prayer for others.

Clearly it is good for us to let God search our hearts daily. While we must avoid what is called *scrupulosity*—an excessive and morbid concern to be rid of the tiniest speck of moral dirt, a remorseless hunt for any spiritual odor that is tainted—we must be sensitive to God's Spirit and acknowledge specific needs for cleansing and pardon. However, the Holy Spirit is always ready to show us what needs to be dealt with and will never ignore us. It could be that the reminder of God's call for our love and obedience was what prompted Nehemiah to move directly into confession.

The Identification Principle

As we look at his confession of sin, however, we are startled. It differs radically from anything most of us have ever heard. He confesses other people's sins *as though they were his own*. "I confess the sins we Israelites, including myself and my father's house, have committed against you" (1:6). The confession is fairly specific. "We have acted very wickedly toward you. We have not obeyed the commands, decrees and laws you gave your servant Moses" (1:7).

Undoubtedly Nehemiah's life was not free from sin. But the burden of his confession has to do with hundreds of years of the rebellion of the southern kingdom of Judah. He is dealing with a long history of coldness, selfishness and defiance of the prophets, all of which occurred before he himself was born.

Nehemiah had a sense of corporate responsibility which most of us lack today. We seldom feel part of the church in quite the way Nehemiah felt a part of Judah. Our culture stresses individuality. We are *individual* members of the church. We don't confess the church's failure as our own. Is this part of Nehemiah's culturally conditioned heritage then? If so, is what we might call *the identification principle* not relevant to our prayers?

Daniel certainly follows the principle. Few men have been more upright than he. Yet he prayed, "We have sinned. . . . We have not listened" (Dan 9:5-6). In a sense, the sins were neither Daniel's nor Nehemiah's, and yet in both of these great prayers, the prayer warriors identified themselves with the people for whom they were praying. They do not pray, "Oh, Lord, forgive *them*," but, "Oh, Lord, forgive *us*."

Another example of the identification principle is found in the life of Jesus. When he came to John to be baptized, he waited in line with sinners. He had not sinned. John hinted as much. Yet in order "to fulfill all righteousness" (Mt 3:15), he stood in a line of sinners who acknowledged their need of repentance. Though without sin, he chose deliberately to identify himself with sinners. He was to be the second Adam, the representative of our race. He refused to gather his clean robes around him or to emphasize how different from us he was.

As a medical student I once missed a practical class on venereal disease. Because of this I had to go to the venereal diseases clinic alone

one night at a time when students did not usually attend. As I entered the building, a male nurse I did not know met me. A line of men were waiting for treatment. "I want to see the doctor," I said.

"That's what everybody wants. Stand in the line," he replied.

"But you don't understand. I'm a medical student," I protested.

"Makes no difference. You got it the same way everybody else did. Stand in the line," the male nurse repeated.

In the end I managed to explain to him why I was there, but I can still feel the sense of shame that made me balk at standing in line with men who had VD. Yet Jesus shunned shame as he waited to be baptized. And the moral gulf that separated him from us was far greater than that separating me from the men at the clinic. Moreover my dislike of vene-real disease was as nothing compared with Jesus' utter abhorrence of sin. But he crossed the gulf, joined our ranks, embraced us and still remained pure. He identified with those he came to save. He became like us. It is this same identification that makes Nehemiah's prayer a truly great prayer.

Pleading with God

Nehemiah's prayer rises still higher. He has identified with his people that he might become their advocate. He stands before God as if he were surrounded by a cowering, guilty nation, pleading with God as his people's representative and spokesman. It may not be evident in the prayer itself, but the whole book reflects his indifference to his personal fate as he does so. Unhappily, such advocacy is the stance in prayer that we least understand.

How bold should our pleading be? Do we in pleading *oppose* the God we plead with? Why should we need to persuade him of anything since he knows what is right to do already? And will our pleading produce anything? Does it not after all share the nature of what Jacques Ellul refers to as "the inutility of all human activity"?

Yet men of God plead. Abraham pleaded. Moses pleaded. Jeremiah and Daniel both pleaded. Paul the apostle pleaded. Their pleas were far from being tame and polite expressions of desires. They pleaded with serious intent from hearts desperate enough to make them reckless in their pleading. What can we say of such men? How can we justify people who seemed to forget their mortality and smallness, to say nothing of the majesty and holiness of God?

But these were precisely the things of which they were most aware. Their God was greater and holier than our feeble pictures of him. Their reckless boldness, far greater than ours, arose from a deep awareness that their deaths would be of no account. Their chief concern was that the world might know what God was like.

And their concern for God's people was born both of love and of a zeal for God's reputation. The Israelites were the people of God. His reputation was bound up with their fate.

Centuries before Nehemiah's birth, Israel's sin over the golden calf had awakened God's awful wrath. Faced with God's expressed intent to destroy his people, Moses could not tolerate the thought that the Egyptians should get a distorted impression of Yahweh's character. "Why should the Egyptians say, 'It was with evil intent that he brought them out, to kill them in the mountains . . .' ? Turn from your fierce anger; relent and do not bring disaster on your people" (Ex 32:12).

God relent? God change his mind? Does Moses fail to understand God's immutability? Does he not realize that the God of the theologians never changes his mind? That he is in fact surrounded by an impassable barrier? That he cannot in his perfection be deflected from a course of action by the pull of a human cry or be moved once he has spoken by the desperate plight of a people? Obviously Moses lacks precisely this understanding. And it is fortunate that he does, since the Scripture tells us that on this occasion "the LORD relented and did not bring on his people the disaster he had threatened" (Ex 32:14). It is difficult to lock the Almighty in the box of a philosophical principle.

But God's change of mind represented no triumph for Moses. Aware of a principle of vastly greater importance than that of divine impassibility, he stands trembling but desperate, between a holy God and a sinful people, counting his own life of no consequence as he cries out to God for their forgiveness. The issue is vital to him. His own life and memory are but dust in the wind compared with the importance of the plea he makes as he cries, "Forgive their sin—but if not, then blot me out of the book you have written" (Ex 32:32).

We must understand Moses if we are to understand Nehemiah. And we must understand both if we are to learn how to plead effectively with God. For what is true of feelings and of faith must necessarily apply to our understanding of intercession. Nehemiah's mind is steeped in Moses, and his pleading in verses 8 and 9 reflect this. In these verses he draws from Deuteronomy 28:64 and 30:1-4. Nehemiah is quoting what God had said, "If you are unfaithful, I will scatter you among the nations, but if you return to me and obey my commands, then even if your exiled people are at the farthest horizon, I will gather them from there and bring them to the place I have chosen as a dwelling for my Name." More impressive, Nehemiah's pleading in verse 10, "They are your servants and your people," is an echo of the cry of Moses in Deuteronomy 9:29 as Moses recounts to Israel the story of his advocacy for them.

There are then three prerequisites of pleading: jealousy for God's reputation, love for one's fellows, and indifference to one's own life and destiny. If these are true of us, we will plead as Moses and as Nehemiah. And it may happen that God would "change his mind" about something as the result of our advocacy. The key is to know the Word and know the promises.

When and where it is appropriate, there is nothing that delights God more than to take his promises seriously. The Holy Spirit strengthens our faith under such circumstances. We find we are certain God has heard and will answer. Indeed we shall discover that in praying we have merely been responding to the Holy Spirit's prompting. We supposed the prayer was ours, only to discover that it was orchestrated by him. Our advocacy has been part of a mysterious pas de deux. We have prayed ourselves into a joyful surprise.

For God's promise is his extended hand. And when we reach out we are startled to find we have touched life and power. We have grasped the mountain-moving hand.

The Mallet and the Fly

But we have yet to examine the most crucial aspect of Nehemiah's prayer. For at this point it takes a puzzling turn. What precisely does Nehemiah ask? Curiously he has not so far asked for anything. And when he does so his request seems utterly trivial, not to say incongruous beside the majesty of the whole prayer. "Give your servant success today by *granting him favor in the presence of this man*" (1:11).

Why so ponderous an opening for so small a request? Nehemiah seems to have used a mallet to kill a fly. Why pray a prayer of such scope for safety before the king? There is another puzzle. "Today" in 1:11 may well refer to a day four months after he had begun to fast and pray. (Compare 1:1 with 2:1.) Nehemiah tells us that he has been fasting and praying "day and night" (1:6) for days (1:4). How was he occupying his time during those days?

When I read the prayer at pulpit speed, it takes me just under a minute and a half. Did Nehemiah repeat the same prayer endlessly for weeks? Or does the prayer represent the summary of issues he meditated on during that prolonged period? Yet again, could it be some final product, hammered out as the result of a sort of dialog with God, the result of interaction between God and his servant? Was it a jewel born in the crushing of his pain and the heat of his concern?

Prayer must never be a monolog. True prayer is always initiated by God and represents our response to what God is saying. We may not always realize that God is speaking. Was Nehemiah aware that the terrible news from Jerusalem was God's way of securing his attention? If we are aware as we begin to pray that whatever drives us to prayer is in fact God's way of drawing us into his presence, we shall approach him with greater confidence.

Everyone who prays knows that praying is more than asking and receiving. I begin to ask and I sense that something is wrong. The Spirit of God turns the course of the conversation. I want to talk to him about Mrs. Green. He wants to talk to me about my sin. I want to talk to him about Africa. He wants to talk to me about my next-door neighbor. I come armed with a list of subjects for prayer. He comes to me with one thing that he wants me to do. It is only in the hours of quiet waiting on him that he is able to sort out the confusion in my mind, showing me how he really wants me to pray.

It was probably like this with Nehemiah. Let us put ourselves in his place for the moment. How would he have prayed? "Oh, Lord, please help the poor brethren in Jerusalem. Help them not to be discouraged because the walls have been broken down. Help them to remember that their God is strong, much stronger than their enemies."

"Aren't you being rather hypocritical, Nehemiah? If I'm so strong and powerful why don't you ask the king's permission to go to Jerusalem yourself and build the walls? It is nice of you to pray, but it would be much nicer for you to go."

Many years ago during my student days, I came across a booklet entitled *Prayer: Focused and Fighting* by G. H. Lang. The author pointed out that intercessory prayer begins with God. He does not call on us to decide on the battle strategy and then ask his help in carrying out our plans. Rather we are to ask him what *his* plans are. To do so we are to wait on God so that he can reveal his mind to us.

According to Lang this greatly simplifies prayer. We would find that just as battles often hinge on one focal point, so a simple request might be the key to resolving vast, complex issues. In place of a list of requests we might need to make only one—provided we saw the battle as God saw it.

Napoleon, along with his favorite generals, had the custom of watching the development of a battle from a high vantage point. As he watched, his analytical mind would soon tell him the key to victory. Turning to Marshal Ney he might say, "You see that farmhouse on that slight elevation above the river? I want you to seize it and hold it. I don't care what losses we sustain in doing so. *Seize and hold that farm at all cost!*"

Lang declared that we must wait on God in the same way the generals waited on Napoleon. I was impressed enough to put what he said rigorously into practice. I knew that my subjective impressions about what God said might not always be reliable. So I purchased a notebook and recorded my traffic with God in prayer.

My responsibilities with Inter-Varsity had increased and were now on a national scale. Deliberately I spent time waiting in God's presence as I brought one situation after another before him. I would not intercede at once but would ask God how he wanted me to pray. I would then pray according to what I felt was his leading. I would carefully record what I had prayed, the date on which I had prayed, the degree of certainty I had felt about his will and biblical evidence supporting my certainty. Then I would leave a space in which to record the results of my prayer.

Often I would be astounded by the accuracy and effectiveness of such requests. On one occasion a serious situation was developing because one influential leader was leading large numbers of groups in a dangerous direction. The issue was to come to a head at a certain meeting, a meeting I could not possibly attend. How ought I to pray? What ought I to do?

As I waited on God it seemed that he was saying, "Pray that he will repent and admit his error at that meeting!"

"But Lord, he's not the kind of man who would do that!"

"Pray that he will repent!"

"But Lord . . ."

"Pray that he will repent!"

I did. And a week later the astonishing news of his profound change of heart reached me. The crisis was over. The tragedy I dreaded never took place. It was not my powerful praying that had changed matters but the fact that I was collaborating with God's plans.

I must not pretend I was always right. At other times I would be hopelessly mistaken about the Spirit's direction. But if subsequent events proved me wrong, I could then go back to God and ask him why I had been mistaken. Soon it would become plain to me. Sometimes my pride or my own desires or prejudices had misled me. At other times I had overlooked an important biblical principle, for the Spirit's direction never violates revealed laws. Slowly I became better at distinguishing the voice of God from the voices of my twisted desires. Off and on

I have all my life continued to follow this practice, filling notebooks as I slowly learn to wait on God.

In this way intercession grew less burdensome and more effective. It became an adventure with the Commander-in-Chief. I grew to know him better. Some very surprising changes took place around me. But there were risks. I had to be willing to take some chances when I asked, occasionally, for things which did not represent common sense. I also had to be willing to honestly face my own mistakes and my own weaknesses. Most of all, I had to put my own life on the line, for sometimes I was instructed to *do* things. That is precisely the situation with Nehemiah. As he waits on God, he is also being called to put his own life on the line.

It may be that a hundred earnest requests collect and wither on Nehemiah's lips before he has the courage to utter the one request that God is waiting for him to utter. He knows full well the danger he runs if as cupbearer he is to ask the king to send him to Jerusalem. Yet finally the words come, "Give your servant success today by granting him favor in the presence of this man" (1:11).

The king's favor is all he asks. Somehow he seems to know that everything else will fall into place if God will grant him that one thing. Often we pray fussily about a thousand details. ("Let's bring every detail before the throne of grace!") Scripture knows nothing of such catalog prayers.

Battles hinge on small but critical factors—the destruction of a bridge, the holding of a farm. A skilled general is one who knows what the key to a battle is. And the Holy Spirit is such a general.

Evidently the fate of a large enterprise now hangs on Nehemiah's one request. Evidently, too, his own life hangs on it.

But in the struggle that culminates in his decision, Nehemiah has become a spiritual leader. The cocoon lies at his feet empty, having served its purpose. God's preparatory period for him is over. He stands with slowly spreading wings, trembling in the sunlight of a divine smile and gathering strength to take flight.

For Individuals or Groups

1. What role do you think emotion should have in prayer? When have your prayers been especially affected by emotion?

2. How does our knowledge of and image of God affect our prayers?

3. How willing do you think God is to hear your prayers?

4. Nehemiah identifies with the sins and the needs of his people. Why is identifying in these ways so difficult for us?

5. Have you ever pleaded with God like Nehemiah and Moses? What has been the result?

6. What is the connection between prayer and obedience?

7. How can you be part of the answer to prayers you have been praying lately?

3

The Leader & Organization

2 IN THE MONTH OF NISAN IN THE TWENTIETH YEAR OF KING ARTAXERXES, WHEN wine was brought for him, I took the wine and gave it to the king. I had not been sad in his presence before; ²so the king asked me, "Why does your face look so sad when you are not ill? This can be nothing but sadness of heart."

I was very much afraid, ³but I said to the king, "May the king live forever! Why should my face not look sad when the city where my fathers are buried lies in ruins, and its gates have been destroyed by fire?"

⁴The king said to me, "What is it you want?"

Then I prayed to the God of heaven, ⁵and I answered the king, "If it pleases the king and if your servant has found favor in his sight, let him send me to the city in Judah where my fathers are buried so that I can rebuild it."

⁶Then the king, with the queen sitting beside him, asked me, "How long will your journey take, and when will you get back?" It pleased the king to send me; so I set a time.

⁷I also said to him, "If it pleases the king, may I have letters to the governors of Trans-Euphrates, so that they will provide me safe-conduct until I arrive in Judah? ⁸And may I have a letter to Asaph, keeper of the king's forest, so he will give me timber to make beams for the gates of

the citadel by the temple and for the city wall and for the residence I will occupy?" And because the gracious hand of my God was upon me, the king granted my requests. ⁹So I went to the governors of Trans-Euphrates and gave them the king's letters. The king had also sent army officers and cavalry with me.

¹⁰When Sanballat the Horonite and Tobiah the Ammonite official heard about this, they were very much disturbed that someone had come to promote the welfare of the Israelites.

¹¹I went to Jerusalem, and after staying there three days ¹²I set out during the night with a few men. I had not told anyone what my God had put in my heart to do for Jerusalem. There were no mounts with me except the one I was riding on.

¹³By night I went out through the Valley Gate toward the Jackal Well and the Dung Gate, examining the walls of Jerusalem, which had been broken down, and its gates, which had been destroyed by fire. ¹⁴Then I moved on toward the Fountain Gate and the King's Pool, but there was not enough room for my mount to get through; ¹⁵so I went up the valley by night, examining the wall. Finally, I turned back and reentered through the Valley Gate. ¹⁶The officials did not know where I had gone or what I was doing, because as yet I had said nothing to the Jews or the priests or nobles or officials or any others who would be doing the work.

¹⁷Then I said to them, "You see the trouble we are in: Jerusalem lies in ruins, and its gates have been burned with fire. Come, let us rebuild the wall of Jerusalem, and we will no longer be in disgrace." ¹⁸I also told them about the gracious hand of my God upon me and what the king had said to me.

They replied, "Let us start rebuilding." So they began this good work.

¹⁹But when Sanballat the Horonite, Tobiah the Ammonite official and Geshem the Arab heard about it, they mocked and ridiculed us. "What is this you are doing?" they asked. "Are you rebelling against the king?"

²⁰I answered them by saying, "The God of heaven will give us success. We his servants will start rebuilding, but as for you, you have no share in Jerusalem or any claim or historic right to it."

Nehemiah is a man of action. Once he gets approval for his plan from the king, we see him negotiate for supplies, arrange for safe passage, do advance planning, mobilize a large work force and divide a massive public-works project into manageable units. This seems to come as quite a contrast to the pious and prayerful Nehemiah we met earlier, for now we see an efficient manager hard at work. This naturally leads us to ask, What is the nature and place of efficiency and organization in godly leadership?

We used to have ardent and self-righteous discussions about the matter when we were students. Some of us were quite spiritual, seeing organization as a carnal substitute for the Holy Spirit's guidance and power. Others of us tore out our hair at the goofs and the inefficiencies of the "spiritual" dreamers, whom we looked on as irresponsible, high-minded idiots. In retrospect both parties were right; and both parties wrong.

Everything depends on how we define *efficiency*. We could say that it means achieving goals with the smallest waste of resources. But having so defined it, we must neither lose sight of our goals nor forget the nature of our resources.

One approach to efficiency is to study the most productive business organizations. How do they motivate their employees? How do they cut down waste? What are their marketing strategies? Which of their promotion techniques are most effective? How might their technology, which has multiplied so many time-saving gadgets, be of help?

The approach has dangers, however. In the world around us excellence is defined by success, and success is measured by out-performing one's competitors in pursuit of money, growth and power. Christians can learn from the business world, but we must learn with our eyes open. Our goals differ and our resources are greater. So while we must share with business the quest for efficiency, we shall measure it by a different yardstick.

People in the world at large differ as much as university students about the place of organization in Christian work. Some suspect it as a usurper of the Holy Spirit. Max Morris, in his article "I Have Resigned" in the *Sunday School Times,* rightly protested "against denominational programs which demand the whole week to be spent attending meetings, conferences, committees, and leave Saturday night for sermon preparation." Some, on the other hand, think that most of the problems in Christian work would be solved if only we could get organized.

But I must make clear what I mean by *organization.* Organization is bad if it does usurp the Holy Spirit. You cannot organize people into the kingdom. When I think of Nehemiah's capacity for organization, I am really thinking of the orderly way in which he went about his task. And orderliness is biblical. "Everything should be done in a fitting and orderly way," Paul wrote (1 Cor 14:40). After all, God is a God of order. The creation is superbly ordered. An orderly God will not inspire chaos by his Holy Spirit.

What are the elements that make up this order in Nehemiah's case? To my mind there are at least three: his forethought in prayer (2:1-10), his careful survey of the situation beforehand (2:11-16) and his task of motivating people before delegating the work (2:17-18).

Forethought in Prayer

The first eight verses of Nehemiah 2 seem to support the idea that God had been speaking to Nehemiah and urging him to request that the king send him to Jerusalem. Nehemiah apparently chooses to make his request when the king has few distractions. The queen is present (2:6) and Persian queens were almost never present on public occasions. Nehemiah is thus approaching the king in an intimate domestic situation when he is likely to be more accessible.

Palace protocol also demanded that the king's servants always look happy in his presence. Gloom was not to cloud the royal happiness or storms to disturb the royal peace. Therefore, if Nehemiah, unhappy but smiling for four months, one day allows his face to slip, I conclude that he does so deliberately. And if he does so deliberately, I also conclude that he has prayerfully decided that a sad face will be the best way of introducing his request to the king. He was right. "I had not been sad in [the king's] presence before; so the king asked me, 'Why does your face look so sad when you are not ill?' " (2:2).

For Nehemiah the experience must have been as terrifying as a hang glider's first leap from a precipice. The gamble to look sad in the king's presence could cost him his liberty, perhaps even his life. He is aware that at some point the king will notice him, and so his senses will be alert for any sign of the king's reaction. The words that fall from the king's lips, even though Nehemiah is waiting for them (perhaps *because* he is waiting for them), will feel like an electric shock.

"Why does your face look so sad when you are not ill? This can be nothing but sadness of heart." And at these words terror fills his heart. "I was very much afraid" (2:2). He has heard them in his mind for weeks. Now they have been pronounced. It is a moment of supreme peril.

There are only one or two ways we can interpret the verses that follow. "I said to the king, 'May the king live forever! Why should my face not look sad when the city where my fathers are buried lies in ruins, and its gates have been destroyed by fire?' " (2:3). As the king continues the interview, Nehemiah asks for permission to go to Jerusalem, for letters of safe conduct and for permission to obtain building materials.

If his sad face was a thoughtless accident, then God was merciful to him and the Holy Spirit gave him remarkable on-the-spot guidance. But in that case we have to conclude that Nehemiah had emerged from the long period of prayer no wiser than when it began, having formed no resolution of his desperate problem.

That is a conclusion I cannot accept. God does not mock us when we approach him. Nehemiah's sad face is his hang glider's leap from the cliff. It is the carrying out of a decision made in God's presence. Nehemiah would not request God's "favor in the presence of" King Artaxerxes unless he planned something risky. And the something risky is his sad face. It is his opening move in being obedient to God.

This being the case, his response to the king's comment is a response he has also thought out in advance: "Why should my face not look sad . . . ?" The words are carefully chosen. He could have played the politician, suggesting that a loyal and revitalized Jerusalem would be a bulwark against the king's enemies. But that would have been both phony and manipulative. Either because he had rejected such an approach or because he is too honest to think of it, he had decided to take another tack. He tells the truth. He is distressed on account of his people and the sad state of the heritage of his race.

Now he is launched into flight. He is experiencing the heart-stopping moment of not knowing whether the air will support him or whether he will crash to his death. But the king's next question tells him that the start is a good one. "What is it you want?" (2:4).

If God entrusts you with responsibility in the kingdom, it is likely that sooner or later you will have to deal with officials—perhaps with highly placed officials—who do not share your Christian convictions. They can be intimidating. Making a request of one of them can be your own foray into hang gliding.

In *The Fight* I described one of my earliest encounters of this sort. In World War 2 I served on an aircraft carrier. I wanted permission to run a Bible study and prayer meeting. The skipper was touchy about his position as top man, and in the absence of a chaplain, he also had the role of the supreme spiritual head of the vessel. I think he saw in my request the suggestion that he was falling down in his spiritual duties. He refused to grant permission. I then stood before him, confused and uncertain what to do.

But our God is not dependent on the whims of emperors, skippers of aircraft carriers or even of civic bureaucrats. He holds all their hearts in his hand. He causes them to make precisely the decision he wants them to make. When we need a yes from an official, it does not guarantee that all our requests will be granted at once. But it is important to have the correct perspective. No official can say no when God is saying yes.

In my case my confusion at the refusal was met with sputterings and expostulations and an eventual order to get out of the office—along with the very permission I sought! I think the skipper's sudden reversal must have surprised him as much as it surprised me. Nehemiah meets with a more sympathetic and receptive listener. But he could not have known that beforehand. How does he feel when he hears the words, "What is it you want?"

Does he draw in a breath of relief? We don't know. But we do know that he "prayed to the God of heaven" (2:4). The plea was no doubt brief, silent and fervent (2:4-5). The king was under no illusions as to what was going on. He perceived Nehemiah's sad face not as an unwitting lapse in protocol but as a bid for a request. And whether from curiosity or from compassion, he wants to know what plea his servant will make.

But Nehemiah must continue to take risks. He knows what he must ask and he doubtless prays for mercy. He replies to the king at once.

He requests that the king send him, presumably as his servant, to Jerusalem to rebuild the city. It is not a leave of absence that he requests but a temporary change of responsibility, since Jerusalem falls under King Artaxerxes' jurisdiction. The city is not only the resting place of Nehemiah's forebears but an outpost of the Persian Empire. As a trusted servant of the emperor, Nehemiah is asking permission to build Jerusalem's walls for him, praying fervently that his request will be granted.

But before he grants permission, the king asks another question, a question that must have lifted Nehemiah's hopes high, "How long will your journey take, and when will you get back?" Nehemiah can answer promptly. He has an exact period in mind because he has thought the matter through ahead of time in God's presence. "It pleased the king to send me; so I set a time" (2:6). He knows, for instance, that he will be there long enough to need a house. And since housing is scarce, he will have to build it himself, even taking materials for this purpose. "May I have a letter to Asaph, keeper of the king's forest, so he will give me timber to make beams for the gates of the citadel by the temple and for the city wall and for the residence I will occupy?" (2:8).

He is now airborne. The air is supporting him. The first danger has been safely passed. Does the hang glider's rush of exhilaration fill him as he finds himself flying? If so, he does not let exultation interfere with the job in hand. Nowhere is there evidence of his thoughtful waiting on God more clear than in verses 7 and 8. He has displayed forethought.

He has planned beforehand. He has thought about everything—safe conduct for the local officials ("May I have letters to the governors of Trans-Euphrates, so that they will provide me safe-conduct until I arrive in Judah?"—2:7) and requisitions for needed supplies (2:8)—and he makes his requests immediately, striking as it were while the iron is hot.

Nehemiah has an organized mind. But if I'm right about his time of prayer, then the organization took place in the presence of God. We are not privileged to overhear the dialog between them, but it will do no harm to speculate.

Nehemiah: Yes, I could ask him to send me. But what then? There's obviously a great deal of hostility toward Jerusalem from the surrounding governors. They could easily block my passage.

God: It would be a small matter for Artaxerxes to give you letters of safe conduct, charging the provincial governors with the responsibility for your safety.

Nehemiah: But the walls themselves—we'll need timber . . .

God: A letter to the keeper of the forest, perhaps?

Nehemiah: He would grant me such a letter?

God: His heart is in my hands. As a river of water I turn it in whatever direction I choose.

The point is not whether such a dialog took place. Rather it illustrates a principle in godly planning—the principle of anticipating difficulties and bringing them into God's presence beforehand. Prayer is where planning starts. Our first goal in prayer is not to get a steamhead of power but to find out what God wants. Planning that arises from and is the product of prayer is far superior to planning that is merely "backed by" prayer. The plan that is God's plan, revealed by him to those who wait on him, is a plan that cannot fail. Real efficiency comes from waiting on God.

If the plan is not of God in the first place, no amount of prayer will make it count for eternity. It may "work." That is, it may achieve the goals the organizers are aiming at. But if the goals are not God's goals, of what value is it that they were achieved efficiently?

In the same way, prayer at the beginning of a committee meeting is of infinitely greater value than prayer at the end. If you allot ninety minutes to the meeting, let forty-five minutes be set aside for prayer. Prayer needs leisure. It must never be hurried. We need time to worship, time for confession, time for the Spirit of God to change our perspective and enlarge our vision. The more time the committee spends in prayer, the less its members will need to spend in futile discussion and the more its discussion will count for the kingdom.

I have found this invariably to be true. We proved it in student committee meetings and in an endless series of board and committee meetings all my life. The more time the committee spends waiting on God, the less time it needs to spend in discussion. And the shorter the time spent in prayer, the greater the likelihood of endless hassles and futile meanderings.

We see that in a few vital moments the future of a nation is rescued. The weeks of waiting on God have been well invested. The king grants Nehemiah all he asks after asking only three questions.

He does so because "the gracious hand of my God was upon me" (2:8), because Artaxerxes's heart is controlled by God and because Nehemiah's replies flow out of his time with God. God's hand is on Nehemiah because Nehemiah has been following God's plan. God has drawn Nehemiah into his presence and taught him to respond obediently to his will.

Confidential Research

Efficiency may begin with waiting on God, but it does not end there. This much is made obvious by Nehemiah's decision to face danger by following God's guidance to look sad before the king. It becomes more obvious as we see how he sets out about his task. Whatever the type of service we plan, it is important to survey the field beforehand. There is no point in building a Christian TV station in a country where people have no TVs. Ignorance of the area in which we are to work only leads to tragedy, wasted work and embarrassment. A woman missionary who arrived in Buenos Aires when I first went there thirty years ago felt rather foolish when she finally realized she had reached a sophisticated metropolis of seven and a half million people. In her luggage the puzzled customs authorities discovered buttons, needles, thread and a host of other things that she thought she would never be able to get in such a "backward" country as Argentina.

Nehemiah was careful to inform himself precisely about the nature of the problem that confronted him. In Susa, when he met with Hanani and the others, he closely "questioned them about the Jewish remnant that survived the exile, and also about Jerusalem" (1:2). As soon as he got to Jerusalem, he made a tour of the walls to assess the damage. "I set out during the night with a few men . . . examining the walls of Jerusalem, which had been broken down, and its gates, which had been destroyed by fire" (2:12-13). Only when he knew all the facts did he make his final plans.

We can imagine some of the issues he faced: Rebuilding Jerusalem's walls will be a two-sided problem. It will have both technical and human aspects. Perhaps Nehemiah knows little about building. But he can remedy any lack of knowledge by his choice of the servants to accompany him. In any case, detailed solutions to the problem of a broken wall will have to wait until the wall has been inspected. Waiting on God does not mean that detailed information and research are unnecessary. Nehemiah will need to *find out for himself*—another basic principle in promoting efficiency.

Although the Holy Spirit can and often does anticipate problems we have no means of knowing about, we are irresponsible when we do not find out for ourselves. Wise missionary societies investigate countries carefully before moving into them. It is not that they walk by sight rather than by faith since their need for faith will usually *increase* once they are aware of the facts. To walk by faith means that knowing the problems, we look to God for solutions.

It does not matter how trivial or how ambitious the projects may be (arranging an evangelistic meeting in a hired room at a university or planning a countrywide campaign). Facts will be needed, buildings will need to be inspected, problems anticipated, needed resources calculated. To build a tower, you first count the cost. To go to war, you first do intelligence work and find out your chances of winning.

My first foray into background research occurred when I became the president of the local chapter of what we called the Inter-Varsity Fellowship, in Manchester University in England. The tiny local organization had bravely resisted discouragement and refused to lose its vision for a number of years. But it remained small and had little impact on the student body.

British universities were at that time divided roughly into two varieties—"gray stone" and "red brick." The former (universities like Oxford and Cambridge) corresponded to the Ivy League institutions in the United States. They were ancient, prestigious and attracted the more capable faculties and students who were more accustomed to taking initiative. More to the point, they were largely residential.

"Red brick" universities were newer. They attracted fewer wealthy students and were over ninety per cent nonresidential. Most students traveled greater distances to attend classes from their homes and lodgings (or "digs"). They spent more time in travel and enjoyed less leisure time than their counterparts in gray-stone institutions. Yet Christian student activity was modeled largely on the prewar modus operandi of CICCU and OICCU (the Inter-Varsity chapters in Cambridge and Oxford).

The model was valuable. Its emphases on daily prayer meetings, Bible study and witness were correct. But life in red-brick universities differed radically from life in gray-stone universities. The activities that worked so well in the latter had to be adapted to a different and less congenial environment. So I began to look at the way life operated in my local university. Cambridge and Oxford were universities made up of individual colleges. Colleges were in a sense strata along which evangelism and discipleship could occur. What were the natural strata of my school?

My survey was neither detailed nor sophisticated (any more than was Nehemiah's moonlight trip around Jerusalem's ruined walls). It was largely a taking note of the obvious. But it bore fruit. It became clear at once that we would need at least two kinds of thrust—one to minister to students who lived in the suburbs and another to reach the minority in residential halls.

An analysis of the addresses of students who showed interest in what we were doing made it clear that students who lived in digs ("diggers," we called them) were clustered in certain areas of the city, sometimes close to the homes of Christian students and sometimes not. They were lonely and longed for some expression of university life. So we formed "diggers" Bible study groups meeting all over the city.

But the small groups were isolated and remote from the university. A Sunday evening fellowship was organized. It was held in a home close to the university, a home with a large living room. Conversions began to occur and numerical growth was impressive. We took other steps. More and different university strata were infiltrated with varying degrees of success. But we always based our decisions on answers to the same questions: What is the reality of university life here and now? What are the most natural and helpful means of reaching our fellows students?

God was not long in convicting me about my neglect of the students living in residence halls. There were three halls of residence and only in the largest were there two Christian students. If a new beginning was to be made there those two students would need not just advice but practical help. I prayed about the matter and God put the thought in my mind to suggest to the warden of the hall that one of those two students live in my home while I took his place in the residence hall. Nonetheless I put the plan in the back of my mind.

I record the matter because in a minor way God's call to me in prayer was the same as Nehemiah's. I really did not want to give up my home, especially as I had just returned to it after years in wartime service. I also knew that I lacked the qualities of true and dynamic leadership. I felt like Gideon, someone of no consequence who was awed by an assignment I could not live up to. But God refused to let me go. Within a couple of months the warden (an Anglican clergyman) wrote to me, asking whether I would be willing to live there and "provide some leadership." I still shrank back for my feelings about my abilities had not changed. But by this time I knew that the command to go came from God. So I went.

It was hard. There was opposition (though a core of rebels in the hall, sizing me up much as I sized myself up, decided I wasn't worth worrying about and wrote me off). My Christian friends did not understand why I had gone there at all. Some from my church misunderstood my motives and accused me of snobbery and of abandoning them. At first I was singularly unsuccessful in producing any change. I got nowhere. No one came to meetings I arranged. I felt alone. Nehemiah was precious to me in those days.

But as in great fear I obeyed God by going from one room to another and bearing witness, so conversions, precious conversions, began to occur. Eventually a group of new Christians made a powerful impact on the population of the hall. With only one exception, the men who came to Christ wound up either in ministry in Britain or overseas.

Good leaders do their own research. Good committee chairpersons make sure of their facts before the committee assembles. And Nehemiah is a good leader. Three days after reaching Jerusalem, he sets out on a detailed nocturnal inspection of the wall. "I set out during the night" (Neh 2:12). Why nocturnal? Clearly because he wanted no one to know what he was up to. "I had not told anyone what my God had put in my heart to do for Jerusalem. . . . The officials did not know where I had gone or what I was doing, because as yet I had said nothing to . . . any others who would be doing the work" (2:12, 16). But why the secrecy?

"Open government" is a political cliché that hopefully deceives nobody. It is true that some democratically elected governments have clung to unnecessary secrecy, even to secrecy about matters that have no bearing on their own political survival. But there will always remain secrets that must be kept because they genuinely affect national security.

And in God's work too there is a place for discretion, a better word perhaps than *secrecy*. We must be discreet, for example, before broadcasting a rumor that affects someone else's reputation. A reputation can be ruined before a false rumor is discredited. The issue of confidentiality is too complex to discuss here, but it will be interesting to reflect on the possible reasons for Nehemiah's discretion.

Clearly it is a temporary matter. Once the inspection is over, he lays all his cards on the table. It seems as though he wants to assemble all his facts before discussing them. And there would be wisdom in this. Disheartened people may have even stronger opinions than happy people. Quarrels are more bitter on a losing side and divisions deeper. Morale is low among Jerusalem Jews at this point. It would be unwise for Nehemiah to broach the matter of rebuilding until he has all the facts at his fingertips. He cannot afford to reawaken quarrels, disagreements and bitternesses that have probably been dividing the community for years, nor to have someone say to him, "Rebuild the wall? You must be crazy! Have you had a proper look at it? Do you really understand what is involved?"

So he has a proper look at it on a moonlit night. (He does not mention the moon, but he would learn nothing without it. Starlight is useless for inspecting ruins.) His inspection takes in the whole wall. Where the ruins block his passage he takes another tack to complete his inspection. "I moved on toward the Fountain Gate and the King's Pool, but there was not enough room for my mount to get through; so I went up the valley" (2:14-15). And he does all this before advising anyone in Jerusalem what he has in mind. It is what nowadays we would call doing his homework. Perhaps he discusses the technical aspects with some of his servants. But initially he says nothing to anyone else about it.

Overcoming the Motivational Roadblocks

At this point he is displaying skill in dealing with a human problem. He is being realistic rather than patronizing. From his long experience in the palace, he has learned how men and women think, how they react. When he meets with the officials, with priests and with the Jerusalem Jews, his dealing with them is straightforward, God-honoring and wise. "Then I said to them, 'You see the trouble we are in: Jerusalem lies in ruins, and its gates have been burned with fire. Come, let us rebuild the wall of Jerusalem, and we will no longer be in disgrace.' I also told them about the gracious hand of my God upon me and what the king had said to me" (2:17-18).

Nehemiah's address to Jerusalem's citizens is masterly in its simplicity and directness. It contains four elements: a pervasive sense of identification, an acknowledgment of the seriousness of Jerusalem's plight, an appeal to specific action and a personal testimony. Let's look closer at each element.

First, notice the posture he has adopted. As he identifies with his people in his prayer, so now in his address he sees himself as one of the inhabitants of Jerusalem. He does not play the visiting official from Susa, saying, "You people are in a mess, and I have come to help you." Rather it is, "You see the bad situation *we* are in." He is one of them.

He also reveals his own intention to act. There is no, "If you people decide to build, we will help you." Rather it is, "Come, let us rebuild." He is a leader who leads, not one who pushes from behind. He not only identifies with the people, he leads by example. And he calls them to join him.

Second, he acknowledges the seriousness of their plight. No good comes of minimizing the difficulties of the task. Difficulties must be faced fully. Leaders who fail to reveal to their followers the dangers and difficulties that lie ahead are not only foolish but unethical. Followers deserve to know. More importantly, they need to know that the leader knows. It is not *seeing* the difficulties that prevents action but failing to see the resources. And the most immediate resource is a leader willing to go ahead in spite of the difficulties.

Honestly facing the facts has a remarkable effect on people's confidence. As World War 2 was beginning and Winston Churchill leapt into power in Britain at the lowest ebb in the nation's fortunes, he promised Britains nothing but "blood, toil, tears and sweat." No speech has ever united a nation more. Like Churchill, Nehemiah begins by stating how bad the problem is, looking not only at the wall but at their vulnerability without it. But he is a man of vision. He sees not only what is but what can be.

You see leadership is an interpersonal matter. People do not follow programs, but leaders who inspire them. They act when a vision stirs in them a reckless hope of something greater than themselves, hope of fulfillment they had never before dared to aspire to.

And hope is passed from person to person. God-given visions of hope are shared, shared by leaders who see the vision with people who don't. But sharing is more than talk. Hope bursts into flame when leaders begin to act. As they follow their vision, clearly and openly facing the difficulties, God mobilizes the many by the challenging actions of the few.

The last two elements of Nehemiah's address, his call to action and his use of a personal testimony, are seen vividly in a contemporary setting in a vision God gave to three men in Winnipeg. It was a vision of awakening the city to the true message of Christmas. They envisioned a parade in which floats would simultaneously portray the prophetic and historical incidents surrounding the birth of Christ, and the witness of Christians joyfully celebrating them. It would not be evangelism but *pre-evangelism*—a prior straightening of the facts. The floats would be professionally designed, and the parade would wind up with a mass celebration in the Winnipeg Convention Centre.

I was among the two or three other men they approached to form a small committee. But we faced problems. It was one thing to have professionally designed floats, but who would build them? Where would the money come from? How could volunteers be enlisted? Should we invite the city's churches to form a wider committee? If we did, long experience warned us that we would soon be bogged down dealing with a dozen clashing philosophies and views, to say nothing of competitiveness and one or two rivalries of long standing. If the vision was of God, we would have to go forward without even the promise of help to start with. We would need to wait until in God's time the vision seized the imagination of the Christian public. So we met, prayed and planned. We established firm principles we felt to be God-given, principles which would guide our policies.

In surprising ways God opened doors for us. We discovered the vision really was of him. We held press conferences, and soon the media grew increasingly interested. Space was obtained where the floats could be built according to the specifications and where inexperienced float builders could receive space, instruction and encouragement.

The idea then began to fire the imaginations not only of Christians, but of the general public. Soon we were receiving telephone calls from churches all over the city, eagerly volunteering to have floats assigned to them. But the high standards were made clear, as were the costs and labor each church group would have to assume as they built floats, or took part in choral and other groups. The call to action, to join in the work God had put before us, was clear.

Our chairman was Dave Loewen, a warm-hearted congenial man with his feet on the ground and God-given leadership abilities. We all worked, but Dave more so. Dave was willing to run risks, willing to act. No aspect of the work escaped his attention. He encouraged, inspired, told people of God's leading. He was aware of the problems, but he shared the story of what God had done. As Nehemiah gave a personal testimony of how God was leading, so did Dave.

The depressed population of Jerusalem had listened with wonder to the way in which a heathen king had supplied Nehemiah with timber and with letters. They were presented in the flesh with a leader who had trusted God, had brought the timber to Jerusalem and who now stood before them, knowing what the problems were, but still ready to get on with the building. His confidence was infectious. And the people were encouraged.

Dave also showed concern for everybody's problems. Leaders with special skills in music and drama were drawn in. Eventually, many hundreds of people, inspired by a common vision, were working together with surprising congeniality. Fellowship among Christian churches increased. Rivalries were temporarily laid aside.

It would be an exaggeration to claim that on the day of the parade the whole city turned out. But a large segment of it did. Later, as the parade wound up for the celebration in the convention center hundreds had to be turned away, even after corridors on every floor were crowded with people eager to listen to the dramatizations from the floats, to the mass choir and the community singing. The Roman Catholic archbishop jokingly suggested he was sharing his Master's sufferings when he was told "there was no room for him" at the convention center.

The pattern has repeated itself endlessly during the history of God's people—the fear and fascination of a God-given vision, one man or woman's willingness to follow that vision, to boldly acknowledge the risks and costs, to share that vision and then challenge God's people to follow. Nehemiah has now issued the challenge, and there surges from the throats of the listening Jews the chorus, "Let us start rebuilding."

For Individuals or Groups

1. What conflicts, if any, do you see between being organized and being dependent on the Holy Spirit? What complementarity do you see between the two?
2. How did God organize Nehemiah's thoughts during his months of prayer? What can we learn from this example?
3. What project or problem do you have that could use some research before your planning starts? How will you do the research?
4. Why are the four elements of Nehemiah's speech (2:17-18) so critical in motivating the people?
5. Which element is most needed for motivating your fellowship or church group? Explain.

4

The
Leader &
the Work

3 ELIASHIB THE HIGH PRIEST AND HIS FELLOW PRIESTS WENT TO WORK AND rebuilt the Sheep Gate. They dedicated it and set its doors in place, building as far as the Tower of the Hundred, which they dedicated, and as far as the Tower of Hananel. ²The men of Jericho built the adjoining section, and Zaccur son of Imri built next to them.

³The Fish Gate was rebuilt by the sons of Hassenaah. They laid its beams and put its doors and bolts and bars in place. ⁴Meremoth son of Uriah, the son of Hakkoz, repaired the next section. Next to him Meshullam son of Berekiah, the son of Meshezabel, made repairs, and next to him Zadok son of Baana also made repairs. ⁵The next section was repaired by the men of Tekoa, but their nobles would not put their shoulders to the work under their supervisors.

⁶The Jeshanah Gate was repaired by Joiada son of Paseah and Meshullam son of Besodeiah. They laid its beams and put its doors and bolts and bars in place. ⁷Next to them, repairs were made by men from Gibeon and Mizpah—Melatiah of Gibeon and Jadon of Meronoth—places under the authority of the governor of Trans-Euphrates. ⁸Uzziel son of Harhaiah, one of the goldsmiths, repaired the next section; and Hananiah, one of the perfume-makers, made repairs next to that. They restored Jerusalem as far as the Broad Wall. ⁹Rephaiah son of Hur, ruler

of a half-district of Jerusalem, repaired the next section. ¹⁰Adjoining this, Jedaiah son of Harumaph made repairs opposite his house, and Hattush son of Hashabneiah made repairs next to him. ¹¹Malkijah son of Harim and Hasshub son of Pahath-Moab repaired another section and the Tower of the Ovens. ¹²Shallum son of Hallohesh, ruler of a half-district of Jerusalem, repaired the next section with the help of his daughters.

¹³The Valley Gate was repaired by Hanun and the residents of Zanoah. They rebuilt it and put its doors and bolts and bars in place. They also repaired five hundred yards of the wall as far as the Dung Gate.

¹⁴The Dung Gate was repaired by Malkijah son of Recab, ruler of the district of Beth Haccerem. He rebuilt it and put its doors and bolts and bars in place.

¹⁵The Fountain Gate was repaired by Shallun son of Col-Hozeh, ruler of the district of Mizpah. He rebuilt it, roofing it over and putting its doors and bolts and bars in place. He also repaired the wall of the Pool of Siloam, by the King's Garden, as far as the steps going down from the City of David. ¹⁶Beyond him, Nehemiah son of Azbuk, ruler of a half-district of Beth Zur, made repairs up to a point opposite the tombs of David, as far as the artificial pool and the House of the Heroes.

¹⁷Next to him, the repairs were made by the Levites under Rehum son of Bani. Beside him, Hashabiah, ruler of half the district of Keilah, carried out repairs for his district. ¹⁸Next to him, the repairs were made by their countrymen under Binnui son of Henadad, ruler of the other half-district of Keilah. ¹⁹Next to him, Ezer son of Jeshua, ruler of Mizpah, repaired another section from a point facing the ascent to the armory as far as the angle. ²⁰Next to him, Baruch son of Zabbai zealously repaired another section, from the angle to the entrance of the house of Eliashib the high priest. ²¹Next to him, Meremoth son of Uriah, the son of Hakkoz, repaired another section, from the entrance of Eliashib's house to the end of it.

²²The repairs next to him were made by the priests from the surrounding region. ²³Beyond them, Benjamin and Hasshub made repairs in front of their house; and next to them, Azariah son of Maaseiah, the son of Ananiah, made repairs beside his house. ²⁴Next to him, Binnui son

of Henadad repaired another section, from Azariah's house to the angle and the corner, ²⁵*and Palal son of Uzai worked opposite the angle and the tower projecting from the upper palace near the court of the guard. Next to him, Pedaiah son of Parosh* ²⁶*and the temple servants living on the hill of Ophel made repairs up to a point opposite the Water Gate toward the east and the projecting tower.* ²⁷*Next to them, the men of Tekoa repaired another section, from the great projecting tower to the wall of Ophel.*

²⁸*Above the Horse Gate, the priests made repairs, each in front of his own house.* ²⁹*Next to them, Zadok son of Immer made repairs opposite his house. Next to him, Shemaiah son of Shecaniah, the guard at the East Gate, made repairs.* ³⁰*Next to him, Hananiah son of Shelemiah, and Hanun, the sixth son of Zalaph, repaired another section. Next to them, Meshullam son of Berekiah made repairs opposite his living quarters.* ³¹*Next to him, Malkijah, one of the goldsmiths, made repairs as far as the house of the temple servants and the merchants, opposite the Inspection Gate, and as far as the room above the corner;* ³²*and between the room above the corner and the Sheep Gate the goldsmiths and merchants made repairs. . . .*

4 ⁶*So we rebuilt the wall till all of it reached half its height, for the people worked with all their heart. . . .*

¹⁰*Meanwhile, the people in Judah said, "The strength of the laborers is giving out, and there is so much rubble that we cannot rebuild the wall." . . .*

²¹*So we continued the work with half the men holding spears, from the first light of dawn till the stars came out. . . .* ²³*Neither I nor my brothers nor my men nor the guards with me took off our clothes; each had his weapon, even when he went for water.*

G ood leaders are not workaholics. They work hard without being in bondage to work itself. They are not frightened of work. They are not frightened of delegating work. A good leader sees work *as a means of achieving a specific goal.* The value of the work is not measured by the status of people who perform a specific type of work. All work is valued by its necessity in achieving the goal. In Nehemiah's case the goal is to make Jerusalem defensible. To accomplish that Nehemiah both assigned the work to others and participated in the work himself.

Delegation: Divide and Conquer

To begin, Nehemiah delegated. It would have been interesting to listen in on the Jews' discussions as to how the work should be divided among them. What part would Nehemiah play in the discussion? His record does not tell us. But from chapter 3 it can clearly be seen that both delegation of responsibility and division of labor had taken place. "Eliashib the high priest and his fellow priests went to work and rebuilt the Sheep Gate. . . . The men of Jericho built the adjoining section, and Zaccur son of Imri built next to them. The Fish Gate was rebuilt by the sons of Hassenaah. . . . Meremoth son of Uriah, the son of Hakkoz, repaired the next section" (3:1-4). And on the list goes for the next twenty-eight verses. At least thirty-nine different groups of workers were involved. The organizational task must have been as immense as the job itself.

We also sense that significant problems were faced and overcome. For instance it is unlikely that work on the Dung Gate (3:14), the Fountain Gate and "the wall of the Pool of Siloam, by the King's Garden" (3:15) would be equally appealing. Yet somehow workers were found for all three areas, indeed for all needed areas. Every section of the wall was being rebuilt.

Workers were of all kinds. There were priests (including a high priest, 3:1), Levites, Temple servants, goldsmiths, merchants, officials, private individuals, masters, servants, men and women. Some worked as families. Others repaired damage close to their own homes. Yet others seemed to have acted in an official capacity in association with their duties. Some members of the aristocracy were noted to be avoiding the work (3:5). But all who worked evidently knew what their assigned task was and accepted responsibility for it.

Such a state of affairs does not come about by chance. People in

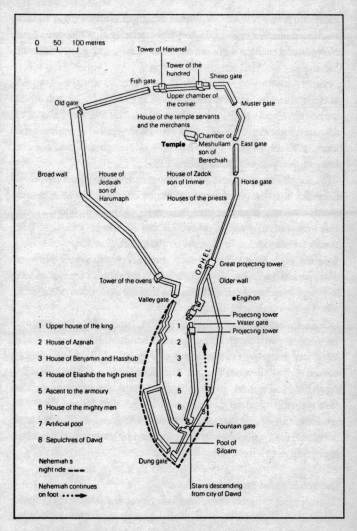

0 50 100 metres

Tower of Hananel
Tower of the hundred
Sheep gate
Fish gate
Upper chamber of the corner
Old gate
Muster gate
House of the temple servants and the merchants
Chamber of Meshullam son of Berechiah
Temple
East gate
Broad wall
House of Jedaiah son of Harumaph
House of Zadok son of Immer
Horse gate
Houses of the priests
OPHEL
Great projecting tower
Older wall
Tower of the ovens
•Engihon
Valley gate
Projecting tower
Water gate
Projecting tower

1 Upper house of the king
2 House of Azariah
3 House of Benjamin and Hasshub
4 House of Eliashib the high priest
5 Ascent to the armoury
6 House of the mighty men
7 Artificial pool
8 Sepulchres of David

Fountain gate
Pool of Siloam

Nehemiah's night ride ― ― ―
Nehemiah continues on foot • • •►

Dung gate

Stairs descending from city of David

Nehemiah's Jerusalem from Derek Kidner, *Ezra & Nehemiah* (Downers Grove, Ill.: Inter-Varsity Press, 1984), p. 85.

leadership have to decide on needed assignments and see that all tasks are carried out. No leader can lead without delegating responsibilities to others, and perhaps there is no more delicate test of good leadership than the way in which leaders handle this task.

Leaders' motives must be right. The most common failure is to not delegate, either because the leader suffers from a need to cling to power or else because the leader cannot trust others. The result is that needed tasks never get done. People who could have carried them out grow bored and feel useless. If you lead, follow Nehemiah's example and *delegate*. Don't do everything yourself.

On the other hand, a leader's motive in making the particular assignment may be to pass unpleasant tasks to others. Fellow workers quickly perceive this and grow resentful. Leaders should be willing to do themselves any task they assign others. Or they should be willing to help those to whom the tasks have been delegated. Good leaders keep a close watch on their fellow workers' needs. Personal power, personal glory, personal ease are never priorities in the minds of good leaders. They are concerned both with the task and the needs of those sharing in it. Such a leader was Nehemiah.

One gets the feeling on reading the third chapter of his memoirs that the work proceeded with enthusiasm and harmony. It is not specifically stated that harmony prevailed, but it is significant that "the people worked with all their heart" (4:6). The record of so many people working so hard and with such good effect must imply something of the sort since Nehemiah had no military power to back him. Indeed his whole approach, as we have seen, was to inspire a desire to work rather than to enforce his own wishes. And he inspired by engaging in the same sweaty, dirty work that everyone else did.

The Leader and Sweat

To be leaders we must appreciate other people's skills and contributions to the work. Security work in the palace would not involve weight-lifting for Nehemiah. We are told nothing about his physique, but it is unlikely that he would be accustomed to lifting heavy stones. Other men would do it better than he. And while it might impress a strong man to see that the boss could heft stones better than he, or a stone-mason that the boss was a better stonemason, superior skills are not the hallmark of good leadership. But appreciation of the workers' contributions is. And sharing their hardships by sweating alongside them may also be.

Nehemiah is not the type of leader who avoids sweating. For him leadership is not status, exempting him from common tasks to concentrate on more "important" work. In his first address to Jerusalem Jews he cries, "Let us start rebuilding" (2:18). The words are significant. The *us* is not a rhetorical device. It becomes clear in chapter 4 that he joined in the physical work and the physical hardships. "So we continued the work . . . from the first light of dawn till the stars came out," he writes, describing the toughest phase of the work (4:21). "Neither I nor my brothers nor my men nor the guards with me took off our clothes; each had his weapon, even when he went for water" (4:23). Nehemiah shared hardship with the workers. His beard would be clogged with grit, his eyes red with dust while sweat would probably leave streaks down his cheeks.

Spirituality is no substitute for sweat. Nehemiah's organizing ability, his coolness under stress and his prayers would have been wasted had he not worked. Prayer may move mountains. But prayer and elbow grease are wonderful allies. They make projects hum.

Some people convey the impression that work is not spiritual, that spirituality and sweat are not partners but rivals. I appreciate their point. Activity, whether physical or mental, is no gauge for effectiveness. The Christian world is full of useless activity. There are rounds of pointless meetings that serve only to keep the saints from getting bored. But activity is not work. Work is activity in the Lord. And activity in the Lord may mean sweat.

Nehemiah refused to spare himself in the work. Half of our problem is that we are too anxious to do just this. We are frightened that we will give God too much and get hurt. At some point we were advised (perhaps rightly) to take good care of our health. But health can sometimes be a peevish old woman. Are you tied to her apron strings? Your health should be your servant not your mistress. Do not run away from work to preserve your health. Preserve your health so that you will be able to work.

Nehemiah slaved with abandon. Later, as crisis followed crisis, increasing the volume of the work, his days filled. And each night he and his followers sank into exhausted sleep fully dressed, their weapons in their hands.

Nothing has ever been done for God without work. Nor has anyone been greatly used unless he or she has done the work of two. It is true that outstanding missionaries and evangelists have had spiritual power. But they worked as well. They made use of the fact that God was with them. High-power gasoline is to make a car run not to keep it in the garage.

Paul "worked harder than all of them" (1 Cor 15:10). Wesley often preached several times a day, traveling on horseback, on foot and in unsprung coaches. Jesus himself not only warned his disciples that "night is coming, when no one can work" (Jn 9:4) but once sank into such exhausted slumber on a boat that even a Galilean storm failed to rouse him. Buffeted by wind and lashed by rain and spray, his inert, soaking body lay slumped on a cushion in the stern. Only one who has worked to the point of exhaustion sleeps that deeply.

For Nehemiah the work came first. That is, it came before his personal comfort. It did not come before God, for the work was for God and in God. That was why he stuck to it when others began to hesitate.

No other way exists of doing something worthwhile. No better way exists for securing harmony and cooperation with fellow workers. "Do you see a man skilled in his work? He will serve before kings" (Prov 22:29). Indeed the one thing all great women and men have in common is the fact that they worked.

Some Christians are confused about the relation between prayer and work. I have heard it said, for instance, that Christian leaders should pray and study more, and work less. Perhaps so. But I do not like to hear it stated that way. Are prayer and study a form of mere relaxation?

Christian leaders who do not sweat over their prayer and study, giving themselves to it as heartily as a beaver to building a dam, will not count for much.

Some of Nehemiah's work took the form of administration. He was a thorough organizer and a keeper of meticulous records (7:5). Some of his work took the form of fasting and praying (1:5-11). Some of his work was supervisory. It was his business to insure that the work progressed everywhere on the wall, that difficulties arising in one area were not allowed to hold up the rest. Thus prayer, administration, on-site supervision, physical labor—all were part of a whole.

The Bogeyman of Overwork

Now while you *can* work too much, it is not true that you can emphasize work too much. Work does not produce nervous breakdowns, despite what anyone may have told you to the contrary. Work as hard as you like and as long as you like. If you're in normal health, you come to little harm, especially if your labor is in the Lord.

Why? Because it is tension that kills, not work. It is getting caught in the Christian rat race that does the damage. It is the desperate fight to keep up a front with Christian friends or with the Christian public, to appear smilingly spiritual and "produce" spiritually when you know all the while that your true inner life does not measure up to your exterior image.

Sometimes we work too much not because the work is essential, but because we are driven by fear—rather than sustained by faith. Workaholics are driven. Work for them is not an expression of faith but a search for peace. Whereas some people seek to be justified by works, workaholics try to keep their consciences clean by working. Consequently they work too much and become slaves to their own neuroticism. Workaholics cannot easily rest; they begin to look haunted when relaxing and turn every leisurely activity into a new type of achievement that must be worked at and mastered.

The Scriptures do not encourage this sort of drivenness. "In vain you rise early and stay up late, toiling for food to eat—for he grants sleep to those he loves" (Ps 127:2). Nehemiah, like Solomon who wrote those words, was deeply aware that labor is futile if it is not in and with the Lord. Nehemiah worked hard when hard work was needed *because he knew God's hand was on him* (2:8, 18), not because he suffered a neurotic need to achieve.

Roadblocks and Rubble

Leaders must be able to spot roadblocks and clear them. They must therefore have solved what for many of us is a personal difficulty—the tendency to procrastinate. Some roadblocks exist because we prefer not to see them. It is more pleasant to get on with what we like doing and forget about less appealing aspects of work. And by ignoring one aspect of work and procrastinating, we create a roadblock.

The rubble around Jerusalem's wall was a ready-made roadblock. Rubble gets in the way. Yet no one likes clearing it. Recently I watched cheap hotels being constructed in the south of Spain. Every evening workers swept the day's rubble down from windows and unwalled balconies to create a ten-story cataract of rubble tumbling down the front of the building. Day by day the heap of rubble on the ground under the cataract increased in size. Workers clambered across it, packing it down with their feet as they did so, and created pathways over it.

Slowly the rubble began to be heaped against the front wall of the hotel, even spilling into the doorways and windows on the ground floor. It constituted an impediment to the work and a hazard. It seemed to occur to no one to shift the growing mountain.

Rubble clearing is a low-skill, low-status, uninspiring job. It is easy to put it off. But procrastination impedes the work. It begins to constitute a bottleneck. And bottlenecks can in some cases stop the work altogether.

While any building activity produces rubble, in the case of the Jerusalem wall there was rubble even before the building program started. Eventually this constituted a major handicap. "The strength of the laborers is giving out, and there is so much rubble that we cannot rebuild the wall" (4:10). Had Nehemiah given up at this point or had he not tackled the problem, the wall would never have been finished. But in the face of weariness he went on, refusing to allow himself to evade difficulties. He and his servant went on laboring at the work, "from the first light of dawn till the stars came out" (4:21).

The rubble we have to clear away before the work can begin may take a variety of forms. Do we have problems in getting started in work? Are we sometimes lazy in spite of our best resolutions? We may already have touched on some of the underlying problems. Perhaps we are standing on our dignity. Or maybe the slackness of others has discouraged us. Or perhaps we are plagued by secret fears that too much work will somehow harm us. Or unbelief may be the problem. It can, as we have already hinted, drive us to work like crazy (to make up for what God is not doing) or it can paralyze us. In despair our hands sink to our sides.

My small son used to work better when Daddy worked with him. Tasks that looked impossible to him when he tackled them alone suddenly shrank in size. A sparkle would light up his eyes as an eager zest quickened his little hands. Do you believe God is in the work you are doing?

Or maybe you are just bored. Your boredom may arise from unbelief or from something akin to unbelief—lack of vision. You do not have a clearly defined goal ahead of you. You are drifting. Pray about your work. Ask the Holy Spirit to give you a definite goal for the next three months. Then drive for that goal.

Or perhaps you do not like the work you are called to do. You feel unfit for it. You could slave at something else, but your own work is too unattractive. Remember the verse, "Whatever your hand finds to do, do it with all your might" (Eccles 9:10). You will be surprised how enjoyable a task becomes when you master it. Make it your aim to do your daily job superbly, and you will turn drudgery into a craft and a craft into an art. Nothing is so boring as sloppy work.

Or is the problem one of rubble? Like me you may enjoy baking cakes but hate to wash the dishes. Spiritual pots and pans are cluttering the kitchen of your life. In that case you should take my wife's advice and do your dirty work as you go along.

Nehemiah did not evade difficulties or unpleasantness. He began at the beginning. He stared the rubble in the face, planning in his mind how to shift it. He dodged no issues and shelved no problems. He had a goal in mind, knowing that God was with him. So he worked.

And through his inspiring example, hundreds of other people worked with him. By a superhuman effort they did the impossible. With no steam shovels or mechanized equipment, harassed by foes and plagued with setbacks, they rebuilt a city wall in fifty-two days (6:15).

For Individuals or Groups

1. Why is delegation so important for leaders in getting a job done?
2. Why do we so seldom see effective delegation?
3. What are the reasons a leader should regularly be involved with the work itself and not just in managing the work? What are some good examples of this that you have seen?
4. On page 59 we read, "It is tension that kills, not work." What is the root cause of the drivenness we see in workaholics? What then is the cure?
5. Rubble in our work can take many forms: procrastination, discouragement, fear, unbelief, boredom or just plain dislike for the job. What rubble do you need to clear away before you can get on with the task God has given you?

5

The
Leader &
Opposition

4 WHEN SANBALLAT HEARD THAT WE WERE REBUILDING THE WALL, HE BECAME angry and was greatly incensed. He ridiculed the Jews, ²and in the presence of his associates and the army of Samaria, he said, "What are those feeble Jews doing? Will they restore their wall? Will they offer sacrifices? Will they finish in a day? Can they bring the stones back to life from those heaps of rubble—burned as they are?"

³Tobiah the Ammonite, who was at his side, said, "What they are building—if even a fox climbed up on it, he would break down their wall of stones!"

⁴Hear us, O our God, for we are despised. Turn their insults back on their own heads. Give them over as plunder in a land of captivity. ⁵Do not cover up their guilt or blot out their sins from your sight, for they have thrown insults in the face of the builders.

⁶So we rebuilt the wall till all of it reached half its height, for the people worked with all their heart.

⁷But when Sanballat, Tobiah, the Arabs, the Ammonites and the men of Ashdod heard that the repairs to Jerusalem's walls had gone ahead and that the gaps were being closed, they were very angry. ⁸They all plotted together to come and fight against Jerusalem and stir up trouble

against it. ⁹But we prayed to our God and posted a guard day and night to meet this threat.

¹⁰Meanwhile, the people in Judah said, "The strength of the laborers is giving out, and there is so much rubble that we cannot rebuild the wall."

¹¹Also our enemies said, "Before they know it or see us, we will be right there among them and will kill them and put an end to the work."

¹²Then the Jews who lived near them came and told us ten times over, "Wherever you turn, they will attack us."

¹³Therefore I stationed some of the people behind the lowest points of the wall at the exposed places, posting them by families, with their swords, spears and bows. ¹⁴After I looked things over, I stood up and said to the nobles, the officials and the rest of the people, "Don't be afraid of them. Remember the Lord, who is great and awesome, and fight for your brothers, your sons and your daughters, your wives and your homes."

¹⁵When our enemies heard that we were aware of their plot and that God had frustrated it, we all returned to the wall, each to his own work.

¹⁶From that day on, half of my men did the work, while the other half were equipped with spears, shields, bows and armor. The officers posted themselves behind all the people of Judah ¹⁷who were building the wall. Those who carried materials did their work with one hand and held a weapon in the other, ¹⁸and each of the builders wore his sword at his side as he worked. But the man who sounded the trumpet stayed with me.

¹⁹Then I said to the nobles, the officials and the rest of the people, "The work is extensive and spread out, and we are widely separated from each other along the wall. ²⁰Wherever you hear the sound of the trumpet, join us there. Our God will fight for us!"

²¹So we continued the work with half the men holding spears, from the first light of dawn till the stars came out. ²²At that time I also said to the people, "Have every man and his helper stay inside Jerusalem at night, so they can serve us as guards by night and workmen by day."
²³Neither I nor my brothers nor my men nor the guards with me took off our clothes; each had his weapon, even when he went for water. . . .

6 When word came to Sanballat, Tobiah, Geshem the Arab and the rest of our enemies that I had rebuilt the wall and not a gap was left in it—though up to that time I had not set the doors in the gates—²Sanballat and Geshem sent me this message: "Come, let us meet together in one of the villages on the plain of Ono."

But they were scheming to harm me; ³so I sent messengers to them with this reply: "I am carrying on a great project and cannot go down. Why should the work stop while I leave it and go down to you?" ⁴Four times they sent me the same message, and each time I gave them the same answer.

⁵Then, the fifth time, Sanballat sent his aide to me with the same message, and in his hand was an unsealed letter ⁶in which was written:

"It is reported among the nations—and Geshem says it is true—that you and the Jews are plotting to revolt, and therefore you are building the wall. Moreover, according to these reports you are about to become their king ⁷and have even appointed prophets to make this proclamation about you in Jerusalem: 'There is a king in Judah!' Now this report will get back to the king; so come, let us confer together."

⁸I sent him this reply: "Nothing like what you are saying is happening; you are just making it up out of your head."

⁹They were all trying to frighten us, thinking, "Their hands will get too weak for the work, and it will not be completed."

But I prayed, "Now strengthen my hands."

¹⁰One day I went to the house of Shemaiah son of Delaiah, the son of Mehetabel, who was shut in at his home. He said, "Let us meet in the house of God, inside the temple, and let us close the temple doors, because men are coming to kill you—by night they are coming to kill you."

¹¹But I said, "Should a man like me run away? Or should one like me go into the temple to save his life? I will not go!" ¹²I realized that God had not sent him, but that he had prophesied against me because Tobiah and Sanballat had hired him. ¹³He had been hired to intimidate me so that I would commit a sin by doing this, and then they would give me a bad name to discredit me.

No test of leadership is more revealing than the test of opposition. Christian leaders can go to pieces under such pressure. Some grow too discouraged to continue. Others build walls around themselves and shoot murderously from behind them. They become embattled, embittered and vindictive. Not so Nehemiah. Nowhere does this leadership shine more brilliantly than in his handling of opposition. It began, as we have already seen, before he had even reached Jerusalem. It spanned the course of his long career so that our last glimpses of him at the end of his journal are of his vehement and competent countermeasures to godless opposition (Neh 13).

The opposition arose from a variety of sources. Sanballat, governor of Samaria, represented peoples resettled in areas north of Jerusalem under previous administrative policies. In addition there were ancient foes of Israel: Arabs, Ammonites, Ashdodites. Some Jews had marriage and trade alliances with them so that their interests lay with Nehemiah's enemies.

The first rumblings of the gathering storm against Nehemiah are in chapter 2. Nehemiah followed God-given wisdom when he asked for the king's letters. Had he not done so, he would never have arrived in Jerusalem. In the face of his letters and the accompanying armed escort (2:9), the governors had no choice but to let him through. But it is one thing to be obliged to go along with the orders from the throne and quite another to like them.

And some governors didn't. One of these was the governor of Samaria, Sanballat. His displeasure was impossible to hide. "So I went to the governors of Trans-Euphrates and gave them the king's letters. The king had also sent army officers and cavalry with me. When Sanballat the Horonite and Tobiah the Ammonite official heard about this, they were very much disturbed that someone had come to promote the welfare of the Israelites" (2:9-10). Sanballat's displeasure arose, presumably, because the prosperity and defensibility of Jerusalem went counter to his own plans. Certainly he had allies among the Jewish nobles, those who served Sanballat's interests rather than those of Jerusalem Jews.

As word reaches Sanballat, Tobiah and Geshem of the enthusiastic response to Nehemiah's appeal, their animosity evidently pulls them to Jerusalem to do their own personal survey and research. An unpleasant encounter with Nehemiah occurs. "But when Sanballat the Horonite, Tobiah the Ammonite official and Geshem the Arab heard about it, they mocked and ridiculed us. 'What is this you are doing?' they asked. 'Are you rebelling against the king?' " (2:19). No attempt is made to be subtle or diplomatic. Scorn is heaped on them and a libelous insinuation made.

People often accuse others of the same evil they themselves intend. This is precisely what Sanballat does. He accuses Nehemiah of rebellion, though he and his cronies make it clear that they think Nehemiah has little chance of success.

Opposition to God's work always has a source beyond its human vehicles. Opponents are driven by darker powers, powers that hate God. This is not to say that all opposition we encounter is Satanic or that its occurrence guarantees our godliness. We Christians are also disliked at times because we are carnal and stupid.

But in Nehemiah's case we are dealing with devilish hatred. Nehemiah's response is appropriate, "The God of heaven will give us success" (2:20). His hope is in the God who sent him. God remains his motivation, "We his servants will start rebuilding" (2:20).

His closing words are tough. "You have no share in Jerusalem or any claim or historic right" (2:20). He says in effect, "This territory is not yours. It belongs to the God of heaven. You are not his servants. Neither your criticisms nor your help are wanted. Get lost."

The lines are drawn. The issues are clear. The battle will not be long in starting.

The Menace of Mockery

Virulent opposition accompanied the Israelites throughout the two months devoted to rebuilding the Jerusalem walls. First came mockery and public ridicule (4:1-3). Then came news of plans for an armed attack by a formidable alliance (4:7-12), followed later by a murder plot under the guise of an invitation to talk things over (6:1-3). With every advance in the building came uglier forms of attack. There was an open letter with dangerous and libelous charges against Nehemiah (6:5-6). Then came a treacherous move to intimidate and discredit him publicly (6:10-13).

With the exception of the planned attack, the opposition demonstrated cunning forms of psychological warfare. Its aim was to instill discouragement and fear. "I stood up and said . . . , 'Don't be afraid of them. . . .' They were all trying to frighten us. . . . He [Shemaiah] had been hired to intimidate me" (4:14; 6:9, 13). And fear was instilled with one objective—to bring the building of the wall to a halt. Similarly Nehemiah's every countermeasure reflected a single policy—to complete the wall whatever the cost.

In the twentieth century we have raised psychological warfare from an intuitive art to the status of a science. Though we think of it as modern—and its systematic study may be modern—it is in fact as old as humanity. As old as humanity? Perhaps we should say that it is as old as humanity is wicked.

For the source of psychological warfare is diabolical. Satanic hosts make it their business to discourage and even to terrify all human beings. But their special targets are servants of God. They may intimidate by weaving mists of horror to confuse the minds of those who work for the kingdom. Often they use human dupes and agents, through whose lips they mock, accuse, ridicule and terrorize.

Whenever in God's work we are assailed by doubt and ridicule, we must ask ourselves where these attacks come from. What is their ultimate source? Is it (whatever the human intermediary) from God or from the pit?

God only mocks those who boast of their defiance toward him. He may correct, but he never mocks his servants, however foolish or culpable they may be. On the other hand, our enemy, knowing our psychological weaknesses, exploits us. He flings fiery accusations at the guilt-prone and darts of terror at the timid. His goal is always the same—to stop the work we are engaged in. Ours must be the opposite—to keep it going.

Smarting under Scorn

Sanballat's ridicule rose out of rage and fear. "When Sanballat heard that we were rebuilding the wall, he became angry and was greatly incensed" (4:1). With smiling malice Satan, the master puppeteer, played one human being against another. Accompanied by his troops and a cast of supporting Samaritan dignitaries, he expressed his views within earshot of Jerusalem's ruined walls. "He ridiculed the Jews" (4:1).

They probably made an impressive group. Appearances are part of the technique of intimidation. Birds and beasts have their own displays, all calculated to terrify their enemies. Recently, while in the north of Australia, my wife asked me to drive a blue-tongued lizard from our bedroom door. It could not have been more than sixteen inches long and was harmless. But as I pushed my foot toward it, its shoulders hunched, its neck swelled and it darted at my foot with a menacing hiss. My wife cried, "Oh, John, do be *careful!*" If I had not known it was harmless, I would have been startled and pulled my foot back. A display of ferocity awakens fear. Sanballat was putting on an intimidating display of power.

In what Sanballat says lies an even greater menace. He asks four questions, each a poisoned arrow of division. The first is, "What are those feeble Jews doing?" (4:2). The poison in this first arrow lies in the words "feeble Jews." For at this point the inhabitants keenly feel their sorry and humiliating condition.

You need not exaggerate to wound. It is only necessary to pick on a truth about which your enemy is sensitive. If you want to hurt an overweight girl, call her fatso. Or refer to a handicapped man as a "damned cripple." Sticks and stones may or may not break bones, but words *can* wound deeply. The Jews would flinch before Sanballat, flinch because they already perceived themselves to be "feeble," to be inferior to their mocker and his friends.

Sanballat's second verbal arrow follows the first without a pause. "Will they restore their wall?" (4:2). In other words, "Do they really understand what they have undertaken?" When I begin to experience doubts about the wisdom of a project I have undertaken, there is nothing I want to hear less than someone who echoes fears I already entertain. A popular song was already going around Jerusalem lamenting the endless rubble and the workers' weakened muscles (4:10). Sanballat's words were superbly timed. They hit where it already hurt.

"Will they offer sacrifices?" (4:2). This third taunt may not immediately be clear to us. He was ridiculing their faith in God. It was like asking, "Do they imagine prayer can make the walls grow?" Were the Jews sensitive about the faith of their fathers? Half ashamed about their hope in God? After all, he had apparently allowed them to end up in this miserable condition. Maybe they secretly wondered themselves if the sacrifices would do any good.

Similar thoughts haunt us from time to time. Will it matter if I pray? Does God really care? Is God really there? You see, if we are sensitive about the apparent absurdity of believing in an invisible God, the arrow of ridicule will be sure to find a chink in our own armor. Potentially it could incapacitate us.

"Can they bring the stones back to life from those heaps of rubble— burned as they are?" (4:2). This last question refers to the fierce heat that can change the chemical make-up of stones, robbing them of their strength. Sanballat was implying that this had taken place. He was saying the stones were useless. But they weren't. They were not *calcined*. They still represented good building material. Nevertheless there is nothing like throwing in inaccurate jibes along with accurate ones if you want to discourage people.

Anytime we are engaged in a work for God, we are likely to encounter the poison-tipped arrows of ridicule. A barrage of truth mingled with lies, innuendo, malicious gossip and implied threats is the normal experience of leaders. Malice arises from fear. And fear is a common response to someone else's success. So expect to have your faults thrown in your face, your folly mocked and your real progress belittled. When this happens, by all means allow yourself to be cut down to size, but do not let yourself be dismayed or intimidated. Remember that the chorus of contempt has a diabolical conductor whose aim is to make your knees buckle. He likes tongue-tied, ineffective Christians and plays on your secret fears and inferiorities to make you one of them.

I am full of fears and chasms of inferiority. Whenever I have listened to the enemy pointing them out I have stopped working for the kingdom. Yet in those moments when I have refused to listen to him and have feebly walked in obedience, I have been astonished at what God has done with my feeble performance.

An Angry Prayer

Nehemiah's response was good and bad. Once again we see him as a man of prayer (4:4-5). But what does he say? The content of his prayer is shocking. "Do not cover up their guilt or blot out their sins from your sight."

Our own prayers in contrast may be tame and conventional. What do we say about a prayer that requests the damnation of enemies? We must recognize, of course, that godly leaders can be upset and angry. We must also recognize that if they feel like damning their foes to hell, the place to do so is in God's presence. While there may be no virtue in demanding someone else's damnation, it may be better to open one's angry heart to God than to bury the anger and pretend to be pious. Better to expose it to God, that he may correct and assuage it, than to pray with correct but phony piety.

But Nehemiah's and the people's anger is best channeled into the work. And it is. "So we rebuilt the wall till all of it reached half its height, for the people worked with all their heart" (4:6). Anger can energize work. It can unleash creativity, fuel ambition, feed determination. Sanballat's bombastic taunts resulted in a backlash of feverish building. Indignation must have surged through the workers, galvanizing their weary limbs to pile stone on stone until the walls rose skyward under their hands.

The Threat of War

But it was not long before news reached Nehemiah that their situation had become perilous. Perceiving that the building was progressing well, Sanballat calls together Ammonite, Ashdodite and Arab leaders to plan an armed attack (4:7-8). "They all plotted together to come and fight against Jerusalem and stir up trouble against it." Jewish informants brought news of the plot. Especially frightening were reports of surprise attacks that were to converge on Jerusalem simultaneously from different directions (4:11-12).

The letters from Artaxerxes provide only limited protection for Nehemiah. He is now many weeks' journey from the capital. It would be easy for his enemies to kill him and to justify their action with a trumped up story of his plans to rebel against the king. An attack on Jerusalem could be defended as a loyal attempt to suppress insurrection. Nehemiah knows that violent attack is highly likely.

His reaction is prompt. "We prayed to our God and posted a guard day and night to meet this threat" (4:9). As in his dealings with Artaxerxes, his prayer is the basis of his subsequent action. He sets a twenty-four-hour guard, stationing watchers with great care. "I stationed some of the people behind the lowest points of the wall at the exposed places, posting them by families, with their swords, spears and bows" (4:13). Mindful of family dynamics and what motivates people to fight, he stations them in family groupings and sees that they are well armed.

The moment is a terrifying one. It is one thing to know that danger threatens but quite another to stand by a crack in the wall with sword in hand and contemplate what you will do with it if a yelling enemy breaks through. Nehemiah perceives their fear. Like a good leader he speaks to them personally and sympathetically. He offers no clichés but speaks from his own experience of God. "Don't be afraid of them. Remember the Lord, who is great and awesome, and fight for your brothers, your sons and your daughters, your wives and your homes" (4:14).

But it is his overall strategy that we must notice. What were his options? First, he could have quit building. Temporarily—until the opposition had grown more used to the idea of the wall. Or he could have considered a pre-emptive strike, a dangerous gamble perhaps but not one without strategic merit. Instead he chose to organize defenses to meet the crisis and to resume building as soon as the immediate danger passed.

It soon did. Once word got back to his enemies that an easy victory from a surprise attack was unlikely, their enthusiasm for the project seems to have disappeared. "When our enemies heard that we were aware of their plot and that God had frustrated it, we all returned to the wall, each to his own work" (4:15). But precautions were taken. An armed guard was maintained. "Half of my men did the work, while the other half were equipped with spears, shields, bows and armor" (4:16). The builders likewise were armed (4:17-18). Watchmen with trumpeters were placed at strategic points on the wall so that reinforcements could be sent as soon as an attack began (4:19-20).

Admiral Mahon of the American Navy during the war of independence is said to have insisted on a dictum when teaching his officers. "Gentlemen, whenever you set out to accomplish anything, make up your mind at the outset about your ultimate objective. Once you have decided on it, take care never to lose sight of it." Nehemiah had an objective. Had he opted for a pre-emptive strike, he would have needed every man that could be spared. All building would have come to a standstill. Had he decided to stop work on the wall until the hostility died down, a dislocation of the work force would also have been inevitable, making it difficult to restart the building. As it was, the force remained mobilized and operations were resumed at the earliest moment. Nehemiah's ultimate goal was to get the wall built, *and his policy was shaped by his goal*—hence his plan of static defense and ongoing work. His posture toward attack was defensive and toward the work, aggressive.

Few Christians have encountered fiercer or more sustained opposition than the eighteenth-century evangelist George Whitefield. Whitefield, rather than John Wesley or any other eighteenth-century leader, was the central figure in the great evangelical awakening in Britain and North America. As a young Anglican clergyman, he often preached to crowds of over fifty thousand people in the open air—without microphones and loudspeakers.

Benjamin Franklin (who eventually became his American publisher), doubting that the feat was possible, attended a meeting to assess the matter as accurately as he could. He concluded that it was indeed possible due to Whitefield's extraordinary vocal powers, his clear enunciation and the total silence that often prevailed while he preached. His hearers were not only spellbound but often brought under such conviction of sin that whole multitudes would weep. And it was by Whitefield that an initially fearful John Wesley was introduced to open-air preaching.

Opposition came early, principally from godless ministers of the gospel. Most Anglican churches were eventually closed to him. Three principles seemed to guide him in dealing with it: never to reply to his critics, wherever possible to avoid engaging in controversy and *never to stop proclaiming the whole truth of the gospel.*

When churches closed their doors to him he preached to much larger crowds out-of-doors. He would courteously request permission to use the local church wherever he was, preaching in the church if permission was given, but rejoicing in the greater opportunity when it was not.

He had an ultimate goal: to proclaim the gospel fully and fearlessly. That goal was to Whitefield what building the wall was to Nehemiah. The slander and abuse to which he was subjected never made him lose sight of it.

He never stopped "building his wall." He preached his last sermon as a dying man from the landing of a Presbyterian manse in Massachusetts. The power of the Holy Spirit gripped his listeners while the candle in his candleholder slowly burned and went out in its socket. He died the following day, his own life burned out in completing the task God had given him.

When you are opposed, remember the words of Admiral Mahon and the examples of Whitefield and Nehemiah. You have been called to a work. Your business is to get on with it with all the strength at your disposal and not to let yourself be sidetracked.

For Individuals or Groups

1. How can you tell the difference between legitimate rebuke and ungodly opposition?

2. What kinds of opposition do you face?

3. What can you do to neutralize it?

4. How can you discern Satanic influences in the opposition you face? How should you respond?

5. What is, in Admiral Mahon's words, "your ultimate objective" as a leader?

6. What can you do to make sure you "take care never to lose sight of it"?

6

The Leader
& Opposition
from Within

5 NOW THE MEN AND THEIR WIVES RAISED A GREAT OUTCRY AGAINST THEIR
Jewish brothers. ²Some were saying, "We and our sons and daughters
are numerous; in order for us to eat and stay alive, we must get grain."

³Others were saying, "We are mortgaging our fields, our vineyards
and our homes to get grain during the famine."

⁴Still others were saying, "We have had to borrow money to pay the
king's tax on our fields and vineyards. ⁵Although we are of the same
flesh and blood as our countrymen and though our sons are as good
as theirs, yet we have to subject our sons and daughters to slavery. Some
of our daughters have already been enslaved, but we are powerless,
because our fields and our vineyards belong to others."

⁶When I heard their outcry and these charges, I was very angry. ⁷I
pondered them in my mind and then accused the nobles and officials.
I told them, "You are exacting usury from your own countrymen!" So
I called together a large meeting to deal with them ⁸and said: "As far
as possible, we have bought back our Jewish brothers who were sold to
the Gentiles. Now you are selling your brothers, only for them to be
sold back to us!" They kept quiet, because they could find nothing to
say.

⁹So I continued, *"What you are doing is not right. Shouldn't you walk in the fear of our God to avoid the reproach of our Gentile enemies? ¹⁰I and my brothers and my men are also lending the people money and grain. But let the exacting of usury stop! ¹¹Give back to them immediately their fields, vineyards, olive groves and houses, and also the usury you are charging them—the hundredth part of the money, grain, new wine and oil."*

¹²*"We will give it back,"* they said. *"And we will not demand anything more from them. We will do as you say."*

Then I summoned the priests and made the nobles and officials take an oath to do what they had promised. ¹³I also shook out the folds of my robe and said, *"In this way may God shake out of his house and possessions every man who does not keep this promise. So may such a man be shaken out and emptied!"*

At this the whole assembly said, *"Amen,"* and praised the LORD. And the people did as they had promised.

¹⁴Moreover, from the twentieth year of King Artaxerxes, when I was appointed to be their governor in the land of Judah, until his thirty-second year—twelve years—neither I nor my brothers ate the food allotted to the governor. ¹⁵But the earlier governors—those preceding me—placed a heavy burden on the people and took forty shekels of silver from them in addition to food and wine. Their assistants also lorded it over the people. But out of reverence for God I did not act like that. ¹⁶Instead, I devoted myself to the work on this wall. All my men were assembled there for the work; we did not acquire any land.

¹⁷Furthermore, a hundred and fifty Jews and officials ate at my table, as well as those who came to us from the surrounding nations. ¹⁸Each day one ox, six choice sheep and some poultry were prepared for me, and every ten days an abundant supply of wine of all kinds. In spite of all this, I never demanded the food allotted to the governor, because the demands were heavy on these people.

¹⁹Remember me with favor, O my God, for all I have done for these people.

Some people are not going to like it when you move forward for God. From their viewpoint, your forward move is a backward step for them. In the last chapter we saw that the building of Jerusalem's wall was not good for Sanballat. So he made his displeasure clear.

And whenever you move forward with God among God's own people, some *insiders* are not going to like it either. The opposition from within may differ in some respects from outside opposition. But it can be just as relentless. It is the enemy's fifth column. The Israelites killed Israel's prophets. Church leaders and their followers have persecuted evangelists and reformers and sought to suppress revival.

The resistance from within may be active and belligerent or passive and sneaky. One might suppose that the passive and sneaky kind would be easier to cope with. But it can be just as deadly. It is passive only in the sense that the people involved have no wish to tangle directly with those who are moving forward with God. But such people still have an agenda contrary to God's. While no conflict may at first be apparent, it must occur sooner or later. Godliness and evil never mix.

In Nehemiah's case the opposition from within was the passive and sneaky kind. But as is always the case in these situations, the passive opposition led to an explosive situation where a major confrontation was inevitable. In the fifth chapter of Nehemiah we find how this sneaky resistance leads to conflict and how a godly leader handles it. The conflict concerns money, people, and the buying and selling of people. Money matters are delicate in Christian work, and financial wrongdoing has often brought disgrace upon us. But important and relevant as issues of money and slavery may be, we shall focus mainly on how Nehemiah as a leader handled the opposition that came from within.

"Now the men and their wives raised a great outcry against their Jewish brothers" (5:1). How did Nehemiah deal with complaints? Was he right to be angry? What did he do with his anger? In dealing with opposition a leader needs clean hands, and the chapter seems to show Nehemiah as someone who may have needed to "clean up his act" before moving decisively against wrongdoers. But it shows him as a mature leader who placed the interests of the work far above his personal prestige or concerns. He demonstrates superbly the principles for dealing effectively with internal opposition, even giving us a glimpse of special spiritual powers that godly leaders down the ages have used.

The workers no doubt derived profound satisfaction from watching the growth of the walls. But they couldn't eat walls. They and their families needed food. Time spent on building was time taken from work in the fields, a fact which opened the door to the complaints that followed. What were the complaints? Basically there seemed to be four in number and might be expressed loosely as follows:

"We have to eat!" (5:2).

"We're mortgaged up to the eyebrows!" (5:3).

"Taxation is killing us!" (5:4).

"Why should *our* children be slaves when *their* children have everything they want? Are we not one race? Yet we have no control over the situation" (5:5).

Evidently the common people faced extreme economic pressure. They had been obliged to mortgage their fields in order to buy seed to produce fresh crops. Some land had to be sold. The interest payments on mortgage loans and the money put out to cultivate rented land made it difficult to make a living. Taxation added to the burden. Cruelest of all, many people were only able to survive by selling their children to wealthier Jews (the ones who opposed the work) to be able to buy grain. And, as is so often the case, those who gave themselves to work on the walls were mostly made up of people who could least afford to do so. Such were the end results of those who passively resisted Nehemiah by not working on the wall (see 3:5). It led to evil fruits because it had evil roots—an indifference to God.

The Angry Leader

Nehemiah's reaction is clear. "When I heard their outcry and these charges, I was very angry. I pondered them in my mind and then accused the nobles and officials. I told them, 'You are exacting usury from your own countrymen!' " (5:6-7). It is hard to be sure what Nehemiah saw as the basic wrong. A phrase he uses in verse 7 is difficult to interpret. The RSV speaks of "levying interest," while the Jerusalem Bible translates the same phrase "imposing burdens." The New American Standard Bible and the NIV use the expression "exacting usury." Scholars argue the case on linguistic grounds. Perhaps the New English Bible may be the closest in reflecting the total situation with the phrase, "holding your fellow Jews as pledges for debt." People were being pawned, and the pawnbrokers were cruelly pressing their financial advantage over hungry and desperate people. But bear in mind that the trouble really arose because of an indifference to the work of God by greedy and selfish leaders.

Nehemiah's anger is immediate (5:6). Does this shock us? Is it possible to be both godly and angry? And, in particular, should leaders be angry? Views on the matter are changing. At one time anger was out. It was an evidence of carnality. But nowadays anger is almost to be welcomed as a friend. We are encouraged to express our anger in appropriate and sinless ways.

Godly thinking combines two equally important insights. The old insight is that explosive anger largely arises from our carnal, fallen natures. It is therefore a foe to godliness. It is almost always sinful anger. The newer insight is that *buried* or *repressed* anger can be almost as destructive as anger that explodes. We are rarely conscious of buried anger. Stored over the years it secretes itself deep in our souls, subtly poisoning our emotional health and impairing the quality of our relationships with other people.

Clearly not all anger arises from sin, or else we could charge God himself with sin. Most of our human anger arises, if we can adopt a psychological model for the moment, from our insecurity, our frustration, our self-centeredness. And God is not self-centered, frustrated or insecure. His anger arises from holy love. Our self-centered, insecure frustrations arise from our disturbed and sinful souls. They are not normal. They are in fact *evil*, as is nearly all our anger.

How then shall we deal with anger? Clearly we must not be so afraid of it that we pretend it does not exist. It must not be buried, hidden, forgotten or denied but faced fully. What in fact did Nehemiah do?

He "consulted with" himself (5:7 NASB). Once again the translations differ, but we are on firm ground when we say that the Hebrew reflects a process of meditation, of reflection, of taking counsel with oneself.

Nehemiah thinks the matter through. He thinks before he acts. His action is based on his thinking. His anger is channeled into action—not intemperate, destructive action but positive, constructive action. We cannot accuse him of haste since we have no idea how long he spent thinking things through. All we can say is that his words and actions reflect a willingness to deal with key issues and key people in a courageous, measured, wise and godly fashion.

His great anger may or may not have been carnal. But carnal anger commonly produces ungodly fruit. Reflection evidently taught Nehemiah that he did not have to be frustrated. The poison, if it was there, was purified. He was to act in God's way and with God's approval to correct a wrong that angered God far more than it angered Nehemiah. Notice carefully what he does. If all leaders handled ungodly opposition as Nehemiah did, many Christian conflicts would quickly be settled.

He goes first to those responsible for the wrong. Clearly he will have to deal with the matter publicly, but first he must make his attitude clear to the offenders in private. This is crucial. It is easy to be two-faced. After all, wrongdoers always have their own point of view and may express it convincingly. Faced with their viewpoint, in our weakness we may be too inclined to "see both sides" and thus fail to express our convictions with sufficient clarity.

But Nehemiah does not allow himself to be weak. His view is clear and succinct. He tells the nobles in private exactly what he thinks. "You are holding your fellow-Jews as pledges for debt" (5:7 NEB). Whatever their future relationships may prove to be, the nobles will say of Nehemiah, "We may not agree with him, but at least we always know where he stands." Godly leaders cannot afford to be two-faced. Our publicly and privately expressed views must coincide.

Nevertheless, the issue, being public, will be dealt with in public. It must always be so. Therefore Nehemiah holds "a large meeting" (5:7) to deal with the wrong. Having reprimanded the nobles in private, he now reproaches them *before the multitude.* "As far as possible, we have bought back our Jewish brothers who were sold to the Gentiles. Now you are selling your brothers, only for them to be sold back to us" (5:8). Because the nobles are guilty and face the very people whom they have wronged, they have "nothing to say" (5:8). And observing their silence, Nehemiah exhorts them to behave as though they were (as indeed they are) in the presence both of God and of God's enemies (5:9).

It is never pleasant to go through an exercise of this sort. A godly leader does not enjoy embarrassing people, at placing them in a humiliating position. Moreover he was hardly endearing himself to some very powerful people. Nevertheless the procedure was necessary if the evil was to be stamped out.

Nehemiah also talks about his own practices. "I and my brothers and my men are also lending the people money and grain. But let the exacting of usury stop!" (5:10). It is not clear from his wording whether he is offering himself as a good example, or confessing that in one point he himself has been at fault. If he and his servants have been making loans for interest, he now exposes this by way of confession and calls for a universal halt to the practice. In addition, he calls for the correction of wrongs in which he has had no part and for the return of property and of the excessive usury extorted (5:11).

If he is confessing a wrong (and we cannot be absolutely sure of this), the lesson is important. In that case his previous meditation would have included a confession before God of his own practices and a resolution not only to right his wrong but to do so publicly. Leaders make mistakes. What marks godly leaders is the willingness to deal with mistakes openly, applying the same criterion to themselves as to others. Never shrink from doing so. You may find it embarrassing. But it is the honest road to freedom.

The nobles promise to fulfill Nehemiah's demands exactly. " 'We will give it back,' they said. 'And we will not demand anything more from them. We will do as you say.' " But wise in the ways of the rich, he makes sure they do so. He calls the priests forward and insists on a legally binding public oath (5:12). A promise made in public can be evaded or postponed in private. And having exacted the oath, he goes further and pronounces a curse on any nobles who fail to keep their oath. "I also shook out the folds of my robe and said, 'In this way may God shake out of his house and possessions every man who does not keep this promise" (5:13). In these ways he fulfills his responsibility as a leader to leave no stone unturned in righting the wrong created by the covert opposition.

The curse itself may seem to us to be both unnecessary and archaic. In fact, it was neither. It may represent what Old Testament scholars refer to as *enacted prophetic judgment.* For example, when Elisha lay dying, he and the King Jehoash are given, as it were, divine authority to decide on the severity of the sentence on the Aramites. Judah has suffered the evil and terrible cruelties of these people for years. Now Yahweh will execute whatever sentence they pronounce. And the sentence is to be *enacted,* rather than pronounced verbally.

Following Elisha's instruction, Jehoash takes a bow and arrows and with Elisha's hands resting on his own, fires the arrow over the field. Elisha calls it, "the LORD's arrow of victory . . . over Aram." Its firing has assured Aram's defeat by Jehoash (2 Kings 13:15-17).

But more is to follow. Elisha next instructs the king to take the rest of the arrows and strike the ground with them. To Elisha's dismay, the king strikes the ground only three times. Elisha upbraids him. Had he struck the ground five or six times, Aram would have been obliterated. As it is, Jehoash will only defeat Aram, but not wipe them out (2 Kings 13:18-19).

To us the thought that God commits his judgments on nations into human hands is hard enough to grasp. But to understand that a prophetic action such as Jehoash's can actually shape the judgment is even more puzzling. Yet Scripture leaves us in no doubt.

When Corinthian Jews resisted the gospel and blasphemed, Paul also enacted prophetic judgment. He shook out his garments, scattering them to the winds, as it were, and declared he was not responsible for their blood (Acts 18:6). In the same way Jesus told the apostles to shake the dust from their feet when people rejected their word, indicating that terrible judgment would follow (Mt 10:14-15).

We fear such boldness. We neither share the divine perspective nor trust prophetic gifts. Indeed we fear false prophecy so much that we "throw out the baby with the bathwater." We think that God can execute his judgments without our aid. Yet it is God who calls us to act *with him*. He grieves over our arrogant rejection of his standards and our loss of his fellowship. On the other hand, we must be most careful not to enact our own arrogant conceit. To enact judgment is a matter of terrible solemnity, not one of shallow petulance.

Nehemiah's actions up to that point could have been taken nowadays by any upright humanist. Calling on priests to administer an oath can represent a legality having only a form of godliness. Every day godless witnesses swear over Bibles in human courts. But to enact prophetic judgment marked Nehemiah as a man who really did believe in the powers of the world to come and who was in touch with God—not only a transcendent God, but one who was immanent and close to his servants. Are we, as leaders, just as in touch with God in our leadership?

A Generous Leader

Any doubts about Nehemiah's financial integrity are set to rest by the concluding verses of chapter 5. In them we learn that Nehemiah's charge to build Jerusalem's walls was accompanied by an appointment as Jerusalem's governor. His first term as governor lasted twelve years (5:14). The post entitled him to levy certain taxes to cover governmental expenses such as the cost of entertainment and hospitality. Nehemiah refused to do this. "Neither I nor my brothers ate the food allotted to the governor. But the earlier governors—those preceding me—placed a heavy burden on the people and took forty shekels of silver from them in addition to food and wine" (5:14-15).

The expense was considerable. Daily he fed about one hundred fifty officials plus visiting dignitaries (5:17). The cost can be gauged from verse 18: "Each day one ox, six choice sheep and some poultry were prepared for me, and every ten days an abundant supply of wine of all kinds." Presumably he paid for the food out of personal funds or else out of an allowance from Susa.

Political appointments bring with them the potential of huge financial gain, and all over the world corrupt officials enrich themselves. Political appointments in some areas put the official in a position to levy taxes for the official's personal use, to make advantageous land purchases and to use governmental staff for personal ends. Corruption often extends to the staff itself.

Nehemiah is different. Many would shake their heads bewildered, wondering what made him "tick." When news of the Jerusalem catastrophe had reached him months before in Artaxerxes' palace, he had not seen it as the chance of a lifetime to win fame and cash. Instead he fought against going at all. When at last he decided, his one thought was to stand for God and help those in distress. He felt about them as a good parent feels about children. His feelings drove him to confront the nobles.

That being so, his enemies could not blast him from his course, nor could riches and honor lure him. He wanted to make the people rich, not poor. Land values would be low when he arrived but would rise as his governorship began to insure stability. To have made money would have been simple, especially to the men who planned the reconstruction of Jerusalem. Yet Nehemiah refused to speculate (5:16). He was not in Jerusalem to get but to give.

Nehemiah scrupulously avoided the taint of corruption not merely because of his moral standards but because he had come to Jerusalem with one thing in mind—to improve the lot of God's people. In the truest sense of the word, he was not only God's servant but a servant of the public. He was that rare kind of public official that has the heart of a shepherd.

Instead of using his staff to pander to his personal craving for pomp and luxury, he took them to the wall to work with him there. "I devoted myself to the work on this wall. All my men were assembled there for the work; we did not acquire any land" (5:16). Perhaps with all the expense to which his official position exposed him, there was no cash to spare for land speculation. At any rate, he eschewed it.

Few Christians in the first flush of Christian service are concerned about "making a buck" out of Christian work. But as we advance in age, responsibility and seniority, we begin to feel that we workers may not only be worthy of our hire but that we should be paid princely sums. Slowly the serpent of greed strangles our compassion and our love. Christian leaders in prosperous countries can and sometimes do use Christian service to enrich themselves. In doing so, they reveal themselves not to be shepherds but wolves. We must be generous toward all who devote their time to Christian work. We have no right to demand that their standard of living be lower than what the rest of us enjoy. But throughout the history of the church there have been Christian leaders who lived in luxury that rivaled that of princes.

They are still with us. And as always they justify their exploitation of Christian people—the source of their wealth. We must be under no illusion about their riches, which are not from God but from greed. And we must see to it that we ourselves never serve God for gain. Let our gain be in heavenly coin.

It can hurt when we see others multiply their wealth. We wonder why we are left behind. Are we like Asaph who said, "I was envious of the arrogant, as I saw the prosperity of the wicked" (Ps 73:3 NASB)? Nehemiah may have been tempted to envy the wealth of previous governors and to resent the continuous drain of hospitality on his own purse. "Remember me with favor, O my God," he cries after telling us about his financial practices (5:19).

He strikes the right note. Our real hope is in the world to come. It is true that God can and will supply our needs in this life. He may even shower luxuries on us. But our ambitions concern an age to come, and so long as our perspective is the same as that of Jesus, our momentary pangs of idle regret will never cause us to swerve from the path of true riches.

The Leader as Servant

Good leaders are willing to serve. Like parents they perform humiliating tasks as they serve their children's best interests. This attitude is key in winning over greed and effectively carrying out the task to which God has called you. The Israelites were willing to voice their complaints to Nehemiah, and the nobles were willing to follow his direction because they knew this attitude was in Nehemiah.

Since the world began, there have been two ideas about being a leader. One is that to be a leader you must show who is the boss. The other idea—to serve. The first idea is by far the more common. All the servants of previous governors of Jerusalem had *lorded it* over the people (5:15). Nehemiah's attitude contrasted sharply with that of the nobles.

Scripture deplores an attitude that "lords it" over others. Peter calls on church elders not to be "lording it over . . . the flock" (1 Pet 5:3). Doubtless he remembers when Jesus rebuked the apostles over their own ambitions: "You know that the rulers of the Gentiles lord it over them. . . . Not so with you. Instead, whoever wants to become great among you must be your servant . . . just as the Son of Man did not come to be served, but to serve, and to give his life as a ransom for many" (Mt 20:25-28).

Once when I was asked to fill a prestigious post in Christian work I was confused. My pride and ambition lusted after what I was offered. I thought these disqualified me in God's eyes. Then in the stillness as I prayed, God said, "I am not asking you to step up but to step down. I am calling you to be the servant of those you will lead." Such was the power of that word that I was promptly humbled and enabled to take the post.

The true leader serves. Serves *people*. Serves their best interests, and in so doing will not always be popular, may not always impress. But because true leaders are motivated by loving concern rather than a desire for personal glory, they are willing to pay the price.

Most persons, while paying lip service to Christ's ideal, agree in their hearts with what Nietzsche wrote in *Thus Spake Zarathustra*. In a leader they want "a strong kind of man, most highly gifted in intellect and will," who with the elite around him will become the "lords of the earth." And the church, like the world, is full of pitiful little people who dream of power. They are laughable so long as they remain small. Adolf Hitler was comical in Bavaria but catastrophic in Berlin. Nietzsche himself was the same. Awesome on paper but a pathetic, woman-fearing psychotic in real life. The Son of man, on the other hand, excites our admiration alike in his humiliation and in his glory.

There has always been a true elite of God's leaders. They are the meek who inherit the earth (Mt 5:5). They weep and pray in secret, and defy earth and hell in public. They tremble when faced with danger, but die in their tracks sooner than turn back. They are like a shepherd defending his sheep or a mother protecting her young. They sacrifice without grumbling, give without calculating, suffer without groaning. To those in their charge they say, "We live if you do well." Their price is above rubies. They are the salt of the earth. And Nehemiah was one of them.

For Individuals or Groups

1. Give some examples of opposition from within that are passive and some examples of opposition from within that are belligerent.
2. Why can one kind of opposition be just as devastating as the other?
3. In what new ways can you be supportive of the leaders over you?
4. In what ways is money a potentially divisive issue for you and your fellowship group?
5. What can you do to thwart these problems?

7

The Leader & Personal Attacks

6 WHEN WORD CAME TO SANBALLAT, TOBIAH, GESHEM THE ARAB AND THE REST of our enemies that I had rebuilt the wall and not a gap was left in it—though up to that time I had not set the doors in the gates—²Sanballat and Geshem sent me this message: "Come, let us meet together in one of the villages on the plain of Ono."

But they were scheming to harm me; ³so I sent messengers to them with this reply: "I am carrying on a great project and cannot go down. Why should the work stop while I leave it and go down to you?" ⁴Four times they sent me the same message, and each time I gave them the same answer.

⁵Then, the fifth time, Sanballat sent his aide to me with the same message, and in his hand was an unsealed letter ⁶in which was written:

"It is reported among the nations—and Geshem says it is true— that you and the Jews are plotting to revolt, and therefore you are building the wall. Moreover, according to these reports you are about to become their king ⁷and have even appointed prophets to make this proclamation about you in Jerusalem: 'There is a king in Judah!' Now this report will get back to the king; so come, let us confer together."

⁸I sent him this reply: "Nothing like what you are saying is happening; you are just making it up out of your head."

⁹They were all trying to frighten us, thinking, "Their hands will get too weak for the work, and it will not be completed."

But I prayed, "Now strengthen my hands."

¹⁰One day I went to the house of Shemaiah son of Delaiah, the son of Mehetabel, who was shut in at his home. He said, "Let us meet in the house of God, inside the temple, and let us close the temple doors, because men are coming to kill you—by night they are coming to kill you."

¹¹But I said, "Should a man like me run away? Or should one like me go into the temple to save his life? I will not go!" ¹²I realized that God had not sent him, but that he had prophesied against me because Tobiah and Sanballat had hired him. ¹³He had been hired to intimidate me so that I would commit a sin by doing this, and then they would give me a bad name to discredit me.

¹⁴Remember Tobiah and Sanballat, O my God, because of what they have done; remember also the prophetess Noadiah and the rest of the prophets who have been trying to intimidate me.

¹⁵So the wall was completed on the twenty-fifth of Elul, in fifty-two days. ¹⁶When all our enemies heard about this and all the surrounding nations saw it, our enemies lost their self-confidence, because they realized that this work had been done with the help of our God.

¹⁷Also, in those days the nobles of Judah were sending many letters to Tobiah, and replies from Tobiah kept coming to them. ¹⁸For many in Judah were under oath to him, since he was son-in-law to Shecaniah son of Arah, and his son Jehohanan had married the daughter of Meshullam son of Berekiah. ¹⁹Moreover, they kept reporting to me his good deeds and then telling him what I said. And Tobiah sent letters to intimidate me.

G o for the top man" is the advice people give when you want to secure a deal from a corporation, or to get permission to do something a minor official would never dare approve. The advice is equally a prime strategy in opposition. Get rid of the top person and the movement collapses. Political and religious bureaucrats have long known it. "Shoot the officers" is sometimes an order heard in war. Terrorists score well when they assassinate kings and presidents.

In the sixth chapter of Nehemiah, opposition to the building of the wall reaches a climax. Early opposition had been directed against the Jewish people. In chapter 6 it is directed at Nehemiah personally. Now the enemy is out to stop the work by nailing the leader.

Leadership has enough stresses and tensions in the normal course of events. But when the leader becomes the target of personal attacks, those stresses are greatly increased. How should we react to stress? How does Nehemiah behave in the face of personal attacks?

The late Hans Selye defines stress as wear and tear on the body. It is recognized to be the cause of many major diseases. Popular books are being written warning us of its dangers and teaching us how to avoid it or, failing that, how to cope with it when it arises.

From all over the Western world, where Christians enjoy liberty and prosperity, I receive letters requesting seminars on eliminating stress. The letters trouble me. They stand in contrast to letters from some Third World countries where Christians are persecuted (and thus under the greatest stress). From these countries come letters requesting instruction on faithfulness and on the cost of discipleship.

By and large, Third World Christians take stress for granted. When they are not struggling merely to survive, their joy in the kingdom seems to make them indifferent to the cost of Christian service. It may be that while we in the West live in an artificially secure environment our brothers and sisters have a better chance of seeing life as it really is. Eternity is a little closer to them. When the skulls of starvation grin at you, when danger makes life a day-by-day affair, or when technology no longer buffers the reality of the crudities of life, one has different values, values less inimical to Christ's rule in our hearts.

Following Christ may actually involve us in more stress rather than less. The call to follow is a call to advance from stress to stress. Happily it is also a call to go from strength to strength.

We are mistaken when we suppose that stress is an evil that must be avoided at all costs. The same stress that kills can also make us tougher, stronger, more resilient. During World War 2, Winston Churchill, the British prime minister, was under ceaseless stress, working constantly, sleeping little, bearing crushing responsibilities. His country could have been invaded at any moment. Only twenty-two miles of sea separated him from the greatest power on earth. Yet his personality blossomed. He thrived on the experience.

A later British prime minister, Margaret Thatcher, the iron lady, is a controversial figure who is loved by some and hated by others. During the Falkland Islands crisis, she experienced the stress of increased opposition from Parliament and the terrible risks and dangers to which her decisions exposed men and women. The international community was divided in its opinions. She herself got little sleep and was constantly having to make vital diplomatic and military decisions.

Yet far from wilting, the prime minister flourished. She adopted new hair styles and improved her grooming. One can either despise or admire her, but one has to admit that she flourished under stress. Part of her secret was that she knew she was winning. We too will go not only from stress to stress but from strength to strength when we are confident of triumph.

Triumph, Pressure and Stress

But it is triumph that is the source as well as the solution to the problem. It is the very knowledge that the wall was rebuilt and that only work on the city gates remained that caused the enraged Sanballat to redouble his efforts (6:1). He and his cronies now changed their tactics. "Sanballat and Geshem sent me this message: 'Come, let us meet together in one of the villages on the plain of Ono' " (6:2). They wanted Nehemiah to meet with them some distance from Jerusalem to discuss the situation together.

A request for dialog can never be dismissed lightly. Dialog may or may not lead to a compromise-free end to hostilities. But we must always bear in mind that fruitful discussion is possible. In Nehemiah's case the pressure is increased by Sanballat ceaselessly repeating his invitation. "Four times they sent me the same message" (6:4).

Sometimes a request such as this may be for more than dialog. It may be a plea to bury a hatchet and embark on a course of collaboration. There is already too much hostility, too much duplication of effort and competitiveness even among the genuine followers of Jesus. Whenever we can collaborate, we should. But when is it right to do so, and when is it a mistake?

Clearly there is no point in collaborating if our goals are different. What point would there be in my discussing joint plans with you if you are aiming at the North Pole while I am called to explore the Sahara?

Following World War 2 a committee of the World Council of Churches decided that it would be a good idea to try to bring about close collaboration, if not organizational unity, between the Inter-Varsity Fellowship (IVF) and the Student Christian Movement (SCM) of Great Britain.

As a student leader I was to feel the pressure of this decision keenly. I was for months subjected to repeated requests to meet with pastors and student workers who all urged me to begin active collaboration at once. At that time the SCM was a much larger movement than the IVF. Often I found myself facing older and more experienced workers whose eloquence and erudition far exceeded my own. By nature I am a conciliator, and with all my soul I abhor conflict.

The two movements had separated years earlier over differences both about the nature and the priority of the gospel. The goals of the original student movement had subtly changed. The Christian Union in Cambridge, where the evangelical movement among students was born, pulled out of the wider movement in order to be free to pursue the original goals to which they felt God had called them. Soon after, Inter-Varsity Fellowship was formed. I was an inheritor of that tradition and of the call to pursue those goals.

But had matters changed? Had the respective goals of the Student Christian Movement and the Inter-Varsity Fellowship begun to coincide again? Some Christians thought they had and that differences were merely differences in terminology. Others thought little had changed.

Curiously the non-Christian onlookers saw the issues with greater clarity than the Christians involved. A group at Manchester University decided to host a debate on the motion, "That the Religions of the World Are Compatible." The SCM was invited to speak in support of the motion, and I as a representative of the Inter-Varsity Fellowship was invited to oppose it. This motion had enormous implications not only for world missions but for the ethos of our respective movements.

Debates were a major feature of student life. The student union was always crowded when they took place. Classes were cut and feelings ran high. Our debate was no exception. Every seat was taken. Students sat on windowsills, leaned against the walls, crowded around the doorway and filled the corridor outside the debating hall. We won the debate easily. Our superior skills were not the cause. Rather the non-Christians judging the debate could see that the incompatibility of world religions is not a matter of opinion but of fact. Unintentionally, they had also laid bare the radical differences between the two Christian groups.

Though it is never easy for me to turn down a friendly invitation to collaborate, I had to do so. There would be no merger. The goals of the two groups were totally irreconcilable.

The call for collaboration can have many motivations. For unity, however desirable in itself, can be a pretext for schemes and power plays, and even a cover for sinister plots. Such is the case when Nehemiah is invited to dialog with his foes. His policy is dictated by a clear perception: his goal was to build a wall. If he quits building to talk, the building will stop.

In addition, the invitation he receives is not a genuine request for dialog. It is a cover for an assassination plot, and Nehemiah knows it (6:2). Naturally he refuses the invitation. But the words in which his refusal is couched show that he has not lost sight of his overall goal and that he is pressing relentlessly and successfully toward it. "I am carrying on a great project and cannot go down. Why should the work stop?" (6:3). He knows that nothing his enemies might suggest would render the building unnecessary.

Let me summarize the principles that are emerging. Success commonly provokes opposition. The greater the success, the more bitter the opposition. If the success concerns God's kingdom, opposition (whether in the form of human hostility or of unexplained moods of discouragement and fear) will be Satanic in origin. Its ferocity will reflect the importance of and nearness to a specific goal.

Attacks will focus on godly leaders. They will create stress for the leaders. Under such circumstances leaders must not lose sight of two things: *the source of the opposition* (Satan) and *the aim of the opposition* (to stop the work). Therefore leaders must remember Admiral Mahon's dictum. They must never take their eyes off their God-given objective. Our overall objective must remain the making of disciples of all nations. Leaders must also remember that stress can promote resilience as well as debilitation. Everything depends on whether or not the stress is a gateway to triumph.

Leadership and Libel

Thwarted in his attempt to isolate and assassinate Nehemiah, Sanballat decides to compromise him politically. He writes an open letter (written material tends to carry more weight) to Nehemiah: "It is reported among the nations—and Geshem says it is true—that you and the Jews are plotting to revolt, and therefore you are building the wall. Moreover, according to these reports you are about to become their king and have even appointed prophets to make this proclamation about you in Jerusalem: 'There is a king in Judah!' Now this report will get back to the king; so come, let us confer together" (6:6-7).

Sanballat may really think that insurrection is what Nehemiah has in mind. And it is true that the same wall that is necessary if Jerusalem is not to remain vulnerable to attacks from Sanballat is a wall that makes it possible for her to rebel against King Artaxerxes.

The letter is not only libelous but politically damaging. It is "an unsealed letter" (6:5), that is, one that will be read many times on its way to Jerusalem. It will be a source of an ever-widening circle of gossip and rumor. It actually invents rumors by quoting imaginary sources of information, "It is reported among the nations—and Geshem says . . ." (6:6).

Under these circumstances most of us move swiftly to our own defense. We are sensitive to our reputations, touchy about how people see us. We are also fearful of what will happen to us should people believe charges leveled against us. Closed doors, faces that turn away, nasty letters, cold shoulders—all these we dread. And more than this there are perils, losses to the work, losses to *God's* work.

In our public statements we focus on these losses. Unaware of our duplicity we say we are defending God and "the work" while our deepest concern is our own reputations. At such a point we must stop and ask ourselves exactly what and whom we are so eager to defend. But our sense of proportion must not be lost.

Particularly damaging to Nehemiah is the lying rumor that he has appointed prophets to proclaim him king (6:7). The Hebrew tradition from Samuel's time onward was that Yahweh appointed rulers, often upsetting dynasties, through his servants the prophets. The prophets anointed kings, frequently doing so long before they were crowned. The anointing guaranteed eventual rule.

The political danger lies in the possibility that rumors will reach Susa and bring the wrath of Artaxerxes on Jerusalem. What is Nehemiah to do? He can go to Susa himself to protest the falseness of the rumors. But if he does so, he will absent himself from Jerusalem for months. It is even possible that he will not return. In the meantime the city gates will remain unhung. Without stout, well-hung gates, all the rebuilding will have been in vain.

Nehemiah opts to stick it out and take care of the gates. But on account of the rumors he sends a message, presumably an open one as well, stoutly denying the statements in Sanballat's letter. "Nothing like what you are saying is happening; you are just making it up out of your head" (6:8). For he has perceived his enemies' aim—to scare him into quitting the building (6:9). And with a cry to God for strength, he devotes himself to his task.

The Christian world abounds in slanderous gossip and libelous statements about Christian leaders. Exposure to leadership, as we saw earlier, is exposure to gossip. Leaders will constantly face the question as to what they must do in the face of slanderous statements.

The question would be easier to discuss if it were always wrong to make negative comments about public figures. But unhappily it is sometimes necessary. Where leaders publicly teach heresy or live in open, unrepentant sin, it may be necessary to warn Christians not only of the nature of the wrong teaching but to name and quote the teaching—and where the sin is publicly known, to name the sin. The necessity arises because the flock needs protection.

But we must use attested fact, not rumor. Quotations must be accurate. And the aim will never be to discredit the leader, even though this may in fact occur. If the leader is a brother or sister in Christ, we must never lose sight of this, but must seek the restoration and the good of that brother or sister.

Tragically, most of the gossip and slander in the Christian world is inaccurate, unnecessary and usually vindictive. All too frequently it arises from pride and contempt for others and is based on ignorant prejudice and misunderstanding. How then shall slandered leaders deal with the slander?

Nothing makes a person more angry than to be publicly defamed. And the danger lies in our anger, for we must be careful not to let anger get the better of our discernment. Who is the *real* villain—the one who wants us to be angry? And what aim might *he* have in provoking the false reports being circulated about us? His temptation is subtle. It is so easy for him to deflect us from our real aim. Too often Christians attack those who attack them. Warfare against the powers of darkness is deflected to become warfare of one branch of the church against another.

To divide and conquer is a supremely Satanic stratagem. On the other hand, there is nothing wrong with defending oneself from lying slander. (Though the godliest leaders have often chosen not to defend themselves at all.) Slander hurts most when elements of truth are present along with the lies. It is also hardest to handle in this case. Consequently, the danger of being deflected from one's real goal becomes greater. Clearly steps sometimes have to be taken to deal with the slander, but we must beware of being so obsessed with self-justification that we lose sight of the work God has called us to do. It is one thing to correct misinformation. But we will never in this life undo the damage caused by other people's misstatements about us any more than we can correct the damage done by our own misstatements. We can go only so far. In the end God must be our vindicator.

Nehemiah's choice was a right one. He responded to the false allegations. In a sense he had no choice. The letter was addressed to him. But he did so briefly, not wasting his time in elaborate self-vindication. He perceived the intent of the slander—to discourage him from building the wall—and he responded accordingly—he went on building. So also must we.

Perceiving Phony Prophecy

The final attack came in the form of an attempt to discredit Nehemiah before his followers, thus undermining their morale. Nehemiah visits a prophet named Shemaiah (6:10). The narrative seems to suggest that the visit took place at Shemaiah's request. Shemaiah is "shut in at his home" for some obscure reason, though later events indicate that this is merely a pretext to get Nehemiah into his home. But Nehemiah's visit cannot pass unnoticed. People are certain to wonder why Nehemiah is "consulting" a prophet. Probably this is precisely how Shemaiah hopes the visit will be interpreted.

Once Nehemiah is with him, Shemaiah tells him that an assassination attempt is imminent and that they should go together to the Temple to take refuge. "Let us meet in the house of God . . . and let us close the temple doors, because men are coming to kill you" (6:10). He behaves as though the information has come in the form of prophetic insight. He does not merely intend to convey that he is passing on a rumor but that his words come with divine authority. The warning is delivered in the form of a poetic couplet, a literary form common in prophetic speech.

Nowadays those who want to play the prophet in church may succeed in impressing people more if they dress what they say in King James English. The poetic couplet was Shemaiah's way of making his false prophecy more authentic, more impressive.

Of course if you don't believe in prophetic words from God, then literary form will only succeed in making the statements sound ridiculous. But if you do believe in prophetic words, it may indeed make them all the more disturbing. When a Jewish prophet tells you in poetry that God has told him someone is coming to kill you (when you have already faced the threat before), his words can strike terror in your heart.

Why then does Nehemiah ignore the warning? How does he manage to see through the plot? What enables him to spot false prophecy and distinguish it from true?

"Should a man like me run away?" he asks (6:11). The question is not a rhetorical boast. He knows that a display of cowardice on his part will seriously undermine morale among the Jews. So at once he is on his guard. His second question reveals a deeper doubt, "Or should one like me go into the temple to save his life? I will not go" (6:11).

Nehemiah is neither a priest nor a Levite. Hiding in the Temple, even to protect his life, would be a form of sacrilege. And when a word that claims to be prophetic violates what God has already revealed, we may be sure we are dealing with false prophecy rather than true. Nehemiah knows that several false prophets are working against him, "the prophetess Noadiah and the rest of the prophets who have been trying to intimidate me" (6:14).

But many habits of mind come to Nehemiah's aid at this point. By now he is accustomed to opposition. He has automatically asked the right questions: Where is this coming from? If it is not from God, then from where? What motive lies behind it? And questioning thus, the matter becomes clear to him. "I realized that God had not sent him, but that he had prophesied against me because Tobiah and Sanballat had hired him." And why had Tobiah and Sanballat done so? "To intimidate me so that I would commit a sin by doing this" (6:12-13). Instead he commits the matter to God in prayer (6:14) and goes on supervising the completion of the gates.

And such a policy must prevail where God has given us a work to do. Fear must never be allowed to paralyze us. In my first year in the university some of us felt we should testify and preach ourselves and not rely exclusively on well-known speakers and faculty members. When the first meeting was announced we learned that rowdies planned to break it up. Fearfully we went ahead anyway. The meeting was well attended. The rowdies showed up. The student speakers were nervous. But stillness and order prevailed, and God did a saving work.

Things were more explosive some ten years later at San Marcos University in Lima, Peru. Samuel Escobar, Pedro Arana and others presented the film *Martin Luther*. Their primary goal was not to defend Protestantism as such but to expose the university to the gospel of Christ. Catholic-Protestant distinctions were irrelevant to students in San Marcos because they were mostly left wing and had little sympathy with Christians of any sort. Their lack of sympathy became clear in the question and discussion period that followed. The situation became ugly and overt violence was narrowly averted.

The danger could have been predicted beforehand. "Wiser" counsel might have urged that provocative films in tension-filled settings achieve nothing. But the Christian students knew they had a mandate to evangelize, and having assessed the risks carefully, rightly chose to go ahead. We must never allow threats of danger to stop obedience to God in the work he calls us to do.

Though we should try to avoid them, injury and death are occupational risks for the faithful Christian. Even universities have in the past witnessed martyrdom. They could well witness more. But our commission is to carry on the work. Our goal remains one of fulfilling the commission. It is not death that represents failure, but an unfinished task. Such was Nehemiah's view.

And in this way the wall is finished. In a monumental effort lasting fifty-two days, Jerusalem has been transformed from a disheartened settlement of oppressed Jews to a walled fortress (6:15). The opponents are forced to see that all along the God of Israel has been behind the project. They have not been fighting against Nehemiah but against Nehemiah's God. And perceiving it they are crestfallen and disheartened. "Our enemies . . . lost their self-confidence" (6:16).

Nehemiah does not tell us how he felt or what he did once the wall was finished. But the account seems to tremble with joy and with the exhilaration of triumph. Stress? It would evaporate as Nehemiah, his servants and his followers strolled around the top of Jerusalem's walls or surveyed them from outside the city. Their eyes would shine and their hearts would lift. The walls would remain as a solid and monumental encouragement to them for the rest of their lives.

We must never be afraid of those stresses that accompany obedience to Christ. We may be afflicted, but we will not be crushed; perplexed but never in despair; persecuted but not forsaken; knocked down but never knocked out (2 Cor 4:8-9). The yoke we are called to carry is designed to alleviate burdens, not to augment them. It teaches us to walk in step with a Jesus who is lowly in heart so we can be released from needless internal tensions of arrogance and pride (Mt 11:28-30).

Though it would be nice to say that Nehemiah encountered no more opposition once the wall was built, his account tells a different story. His commission from God was far more comprehensive than that of merely rebuilding the defenses of Jerusalem. The wall was merely the first step in the rebuilding of a nation. And along with Ezra, Nehemiah was to lay foundations for national reforms that would continue to make their impact felt for more than four centuries—until the coming of Christ.

Opposition would never be the same again. It would be more low key, though nonetheless deadly. It would come more from "friends" than from enemies. Already it was beginning. Tobiah the fox was already busily trying to establish himself as an influential member of the Jewish community. He perceived that Nehemiah had come to stay. His connections with Sanballat will therefore be an embarrassment, and so his marriage alliances among the Jews will be stressed. Busily he sets to work to mend fences with Nehemiah (6:17-19). We shall have occasion to discuss Tobiah in more detail later.

The School of Courage

I cannot conclude this chapter without commenting again on Nehemiah's courage. "Should a man like me run away?" (6:11). The words echo across the centuries to us. Like Nehemiah we live in days when we must let our courage be seen by the way we act and speak. It will help us, perhaps, to realize that true courage does not consist in the absence of fear but in doing what God wants even when we are afraid, disturbed and hurt.

This was true of Nehemiah. Long before the task in Jerusalem began, as he faced the question of making his first request to Artaxerxes, Nehemiah confessed, "I was . . . afraid" (2:2). He probably experienced fear many times in his life, but at the start of the story he established the habit that became of real service to him later—moving ahead in spite of fear.

It was in that moment that he enrolled in God's school of courage. He graduated with honors from the same school when months later he declared, "Should a man like me run away?"

It is a tough school. Thousands of leaders down the ages have taken the course. There are practical classes in opposition, in difficult circumstances, in loneliness, misunderstanding and tribulation. Some students quit because classes are so rough, not realizing their value. There are no entrance qualifications. Any Christian may apply for training. And the Principal himself is available for interviews with every prospective student, at any hour of the day. You have only to knock and you will be admitted into his office.

For Individuals or Groups

1. What situations do you know of where an organization or a work disintegrated when the leader or leaders were taken out of the picture?
2. What is an appropriate response to the stress you feel as a Christian leader?
3. How are rumors and gossip destructive of a leader and what a leader is trying to achieve?
4. How should you respond to slander?
5. How can you tell if advice you receive from others comes from God or not?
6. Courage is not lack of fear but moving ahead in spite of fear. What fears do you face? How can you move ahead in spite of them?

8

The
Leader &
Renewal

8 ALL THE PEOPLE ASSEMBLED AS ONE MAN IN THE SQUARE BEFORE THE WATER Gate. They told Ezra the scribe to bring out the Book of the Law of Moses, which the LORD had commanded for Israel.

²So on the first day of the seventh month Ezra the priest brought the Law before the assembly, which was made up of men and women and all who were able to understand. ³He read it aloud from daybreak till noon as he faced the square before the Water Gate in the presence of the men, women and others who could understand. And all the people listened attentively to the Book of the Law.

⁴Ezra the scribe stood on a high wooden platform built for the occasion. Beside him on his right stood Mattithiah, Shema, Anaiah, Uriah, Hilkiah and Maaseiah; and on his left were Pedaiah, Mishael, Malkijah, Hashum, Hashbaddanah, Zechariah and Meshullam.

⁵Ezra opened the book. All the people could see him because he was standing above them; and as he opened it, the people all stood up. ⁶Ezra praised the LORD, the great God; and all the people lifted their hands and responded, "Amen! Amen!" Then they bowed down and worshiped the LORD with their faces to the ground.

⁷The Levites—Jeshua, Bani, Sherebiah, Jamin, Akkub, Shabbethai, Hodiah, Maaseiah, Kelita, Azariah, Jozabad, Hanan and Pelaiah—instruct-

ed the people in the Law while the people were standing there. ⁸They read
from the Book of the Law of God, making it clear and giving the meaning so that the people could understand what was being read.

⁹Then Nehemiah the governor, Ezra the priest and scribe, and the
Levites who were instructing the people said to them all, "This day is
sacred to the LORD your God. Do not mourn or weep." For all the people
had been weeping as they listened to the words of the Law.

¹⁰Nehemiah said, "Go and enjoy choice food and sweet drinks, and
send some to those who have nothing prepared. This day is sacred to our
Lord. Do not grieve, for the joy of the LORD is your strength."

¹¹The Levites calmed all the people, saying, "Be still, for this is a sacred
day. Do not grieve."

¹²Then all the people went away to eat and drink, to send portions
of food and to celebrate with great joy, because they now understood
the words that had been made known to them.

¹³On the second day of the month, the heads of all the families, along
with the priests and the Levites, gathered around Ezra the scribe to give
attention to the words of the Law. ¹⁴They found written in the Law,
which the LORD had commanded through Moses, that the Israelites were
to live in booths during the feast of the seventh month ¹⁵and that they
should proclaim this word and spread it throughout their towns and in
Jerusalem: "Go out into the hill country and bring back branches from
olive and wild olive trees, and from myrtles, palms and shade trees, to
make booths"—as it is written.

¹⁶So the people went out and brought back branches and built themselves booths on their own roofs, in their courtyards, in the courts of the
house of God and in the square by the Water Gate and the one by the
Gate of Ephraim. ¹⁷The whole company that had returned from exile
built booths and lived in them. From the days of Joshua son of Nun until
that day, the Israelites had not celebrated it like this. And their joy was
very great.

¹⁸Day after day, from the first day to the last, Ezra read from the Book
of the Law of God. They celebrated the feast for seven days, and on the
eighth day, in accordance with the regulation, there was an assembly.

9 *On the twenty-fourth day of the same month, the Israelites gathered together, fasting and wearing sackcloth and having dust on their heads. ²Those of Israelite descent had separated themselves from all foreigners. They stood in their places and confessed their sins and the wickedness of their fathers. ³They stood where they were and read from the Book of the Law of the LORD their God for a quarter of the day, and spent another quarter in confession and in worshiping the LORD their God. ⁴Standing on the stairs were the Levites—Jeshua, Bani, Kadmiel, Shebaniah, Bunni, Sherebiah, Bani and Kenani—who called with loud voices to the LORD their God. ⁵And the Levites—Jeshua, Kadmiel, Bani, Hashabneiah, Sherebiah, Hodiah, Shebaniah and Pethahiah—said: "Stand up and praise the LORD your God, who is from everlasting to everlasting."*

From time to time the church is astounded and the world stunned when revival in the former gives rise to an awakening in the latter. Preaching may play its part, but everybody present agrees that only the power of God can account for the extraordinary things that take place.

The revival in the Hebrides off northwest Scotland during the 1940s is a good example. Following a fairly standard opening address in a church by Donald Campbell, a visiting evangelist, a teen-age boy rose to utter a lengthy prayer. As he prayed, staid Presbyterian men and women fell to the ground under terrible conviction of sin. It was the beginning of weeks and months of conviction, conversion and renewal among the Hebridean islanders. Fishermen passing the island in their boats would be overcome by a sense of sin so that they were constrained to pull into the harbor to find relief there. Whole shifts of below-the-ground miners would be too distressed to continue their work until they had resolved their relationship with God. Events of this sort can only be explained supernaturally.

Revival interests Christians deeply. Charles Finney, a New England revivalist, taught that it would always follow when God's people called upon him in deeply repentant faith. Other teachers insist that revival cannot depend on human initiative but always comes as a sovereign act of God.

Something in the nature of revival is described in the eighth chapter of Nehemiah. Its effects were lasting. And the revival was followed by a powerful movement for reform. While it may not be possible for us to understand everything about revival, surely we should look at Nehemiah 8—9 to learn what we can. In particular we should look at the interaction between godly leadership, revival and reformation.

The Beginnings of Renewal

How was it that the southern kingdom of Judah survived after the captivity in Babylon? Like the northern kingdom, it so easily could have been dispersed like mist before the winds of history. Instead, the tiny group of survivors around Jerusalem became a nation which two and a half millennia later still remains prominent in the theater of world events. Nehemiah's leadership helped bring this about. Although he is known for the rebuilding of Jerusalem's wall, his greatest contribution was to rebuild a nation or at least to lay down solid foundations for that rebuilding.

The beginning had already been made before Nehemiah arrived in Jerusalem. Years before, the earliest waves of returned captives had made their priorities clear when they rebuilt the altar on the old Temple site in Jerusalem (Ezra 3:3). The rebuilt Temple was completed in 520 B.C., seventy years after the fall of Jerusalem. Then, fifty-eight years after the Temple had been rebuilt and thirteen years before Nehemiah reached Jerusalem, Ezra the scribe arrived.

Ezra was a man with unusual ambition. His aim in life was to study, to practice and to teach God's laws. His ambition thus included *doing* (Ezra 7:10). It was this that made him unusual. Many preachers aim to study and teach. But their study and teaching is not centered in a desire to *do* the Word and will of God.

Thoroughgoing reform was needed among the returned captives. Ezra's life and teaching, along with Nehemiah's leadership, were instrumental in shaping the reform. The books of Ezra and Nehemiah reflect the struggles and conflicts that were involved. But in the eighth chapter of Nehemiah we read of something quite extraordinary, a spiritual renewal or revival. What was its nature? How did it come about? Are there lessons in this ancient revival for us today?

Spontaneously the people pour into the Water Gate square requesting Ezra to give them a reading of Scripture (8:1). They do not gather in response to organized publicity. The narrative gives no explanation for their request. We may assume the Holy Spirit is behind it and that prayer has played some part. But it is likely that the Holy Spirit has used the examples of Ezra and Nehemiah to awaken a hunger and a curiosity.

In many ways very different, both men had in common a radical commitment to obey God and his Word. We have many experts in the knowledge and communication of Scripture, and a disproportionate intellectual preoccupation with the minutiae of biblical content. We lack teachers whose lives exemplify radical and sacrificial obedience, something commonly accompanied by manifestations of divine power—and something that marked two such diverse leaders as Ezra the scholar and Nehemiah the man of action and the governor.

We assume that the power of God manifested through these remarkable men had stirred in the people a hunger to know more. A picture, they say, is worth a thousand words. Nehemiah has provided a dramatic demonstration of the power of God. The walls are proof of that power. And Nehemiah's open commitment to godly principles is linked in people's minds with the miracle of the walls.

A vast crowd collects at the Water Gate. Ezra is (by custom?) at the Water Gate. And the crowd demands that he bring the book of Moses. The book's contents, they seem to feel, are not only for the benefit of the priestly caste, but for all the people of Israel.

The Place of Spiritual Understanding

We are told twice in the next few verses that the crowd was made up of people who were able to understand (8:2-3). Then we are told the arrangements for the reading were designed "so that the people could understand what was being read" (8:8).

This is important. It is important because following the reading there was a dramatic emotional reaction. Spontaneously the crowd broke into lamentation and weeping. "The Levites . . . read from the Book of the Law of God, making it clear and giving the meaning so that the people could understand what was being read. Then Nehemiah the governor, Ezra the priest and scribe, and the Levites . . . said to them all, 'This day is sacred to the LORD your God. Do not mourn or weep.' For all the people had been weeping as they listened to the words of the Law" (8:7-9). In this incident can we find a model for renewal?

In modern meetings, crowd expectations, music, the content of messages, the setting, the expertise of the leaders all play a part in determining the way the audience reacts. Yet in this case there seems to be little doubt that it was the understanding of the people that led to the emotional reaction.

Take the reading arrangement, for example. Flanking Ezra's pulpit on both sides were Levites whose job was to explain the things Ezra read (8:4). To us the arrangement may seem clumsy. The crowd was huge and the Levites may have been stationed at some distance from one another and Ezra. They may have had the function of repeating the words for the benefit of those who could not hear. But they certainly had the function of interpreting and explaining the words that Ezra read to the crowd.

It seems clear that *when the Holy Spirit opened the people's understanding* the reaction followed. The only other possible explanation would have involved psychological manipulation on the part of Ezra and Nehemiah. However, the arrangement described above does not lend itself to this. Indeed Ezra and Nehemiah were distressed by the weeping. In alarm they and Levites strove to calm the people, pointing out that rejoicing would be more appropriate than distress. In place of weeping they called for feasting and celebration because the Word of God had come to the people again. "Nehemiah said, 'Go and enjoy choice food and sweet drinks, and send some to those who have nothing prepared. This day is sacred to our Lord. Do not grieve, for the joy of the LORD is your strength' " (8:10).

Can you conceive modern organizers of a revival meeting behaving in such a manner? We feel we have it made when people begin to weep! And this may be because we are more concerned with visible results than with inner enlightenment.

Unfortunately, we can make people weep in the meeting by psychological techniques. (I have described how it can be done in *The Golden Cow.*) Many preachers use psychological manipulation without altogether realizing they are doing so. It is gratifying to perceive a powerful emotion gripping a congregation. We too easily jump to the conclusion that God is at work when in fact this may not be the case at all. This is why so much sterility follows powerful meetings: the power is sometimes psychological and not spiritual. Psychological manipulation cannot produce ongoing spiritual renewal. Spiritual change can. But spiritual change is always associated with spiritual understanding.

Preachers fall into the habit of unwittingly applying psychological pressure when they lose confidence in the power of God's Word. Our duty is to impart understanding. And when the results become more important to us than understanding, we are inclined to take matters into our own hands and manipulate people.

Change is brought about in human beings in a distinct order. The sequence is understanding, conscience, emotion and then volition. Not all these faculties may be equally affected. Usually *understanding* God's Word produces some activity of *conscience.* Either we feel our guilt or else we rejoice in God's free pardon. A disturbed *conscience* leads to distressed *emotions.* A clear conscience, on the other hand, leads to peaceful emotions.

Distressed *emotions* may then lead to *volitional changes.* When I am frightened I may flee or fight. My emotions incline me to take some action. Hence, knowing I am guilty (understanding and conscience) awakens distress and fear in me (emotions) which may cause me to repent and believe (volition).

Paul was aware of this sequence. "We have renounced the things hidden . . . not walking in craftiness or adulterating the word of God, but by the manifestation of truth commending ourselves to every man's conscience in the sight of God" (2 Cor 4:2 NASB). He presented truth to people's minds so that their consciences could come to grips with it.

Paul is aware, as the verses following his statement make plain, that the battle for understanding is a spiritual battle. We shall look at this more carefully in a moment. For the present we must settle it in our minds that our duty is to inform, to teach, to impart understanding. The Spirit is to do the rest.

Nonetheless, understanding that is merely intellectual is incomplete understanding. Psychoanalysts are aware of this. They talk about *insight,* that special kind of understanding that releases from bondage, that awakens, that changes lives. You can "understand" something, even express that something in words, without it having the power to change you. Many Christians buy books "explaining" spiritual secrets. They can repeat the explanations they have read and profess to believe them and yet know little or nothing of the power that changes. Where, then, does true spiritual understanding come from?

Reverence and respect predispose us to understand. The people at the Water Gate wanted to know. They perceived in Ezra and Nehemiah something more potent than they themselves possessed. They also perceived that the power had to do with the Word of God that was recorded on a scroll Ezra had. Their God was Yahweh the Creator. Their respect for this God, and consequently for his recorded words, had grown as a result of their contact with Ezra and Nehemiah.

So when they see Ezra unrolling the scroll, they scramble to their feet with respect. And as Ezra prays they cry out their "amens" and raise their hands. They then prostrate themselves, faces to the dust (8:5-6). They sense they are in the presence of God. They wait expectantly for him to speak. Respect and reverence for God predisposed them—and will predispose us—to understand what God has to say. Respect for Scripture is valueless unless it springs from awe of the God of Scripture.

What causes their distress? Probably the realization of how far they have fallen short of God's instructions. The grief is real grief over their shortcomings. It is not a form of self-pity, for self-pity cannot easily be turned into rejoicing. Ezra and Nehemiah are successful in encouraging the people to rejoice. Wholesome, healthy grief over sin is never far from joy, for it is always provoked by a God of mercy and salvation. Soon a celebration is under way. "Then all the people went away to eat and drink, to send portions of food and to celebrate with great joy, because they now understood the words that had been made known to them" (8:12).

The Results of Renewal

The renewal begins as men and women break down and weep over their disobedience. It is followed immediately by a spontaneous reforming zeal on the part of the populace as a whole. The order is significant—spiritual renewal first followed by reform. When repentance and new life occur, reformation follows.

One result of genuine renewal is a quickened interest in and grasp of Scripture. Revived people delight in it. They become eager to practice it. Renewal produces changed lives and changed societies. The genuineness and extent of the renewal can be assessed by the societal reforms resulting from it. Mere religious excitement does not produce beneficial social change. True revival does.

The immediate effects in Jerusalem are dramatic but may not at once seem all that significant. The people become interested in the Feast of Booths (8:13-17). The history of the feast goes back to their earliest days in the Promised Land. It was designed so that the Israelites would never forget that their ancestors had lived in tents in the wilderness. Once having reached the Promised Land and having tasted its fruits, they were to make booths of branches and palm fronds at harvest time and to live in them for a week (Lev 23:33-43).

It was their form of harvest festival. By re-enacting the old existence with the fruits of the new, the contrast between what had been and what now was would be reinforced. The people's dependence on and gratitude to God would be reawakened.

The Feast of Booths was both a festival and a ceremony. In Nehemiah's day the festival and the ceremony made them aware not only of

God but of their history, their roots, and of what and who they were. There would be a lifting of their morale and a restoration of their dignity as a people. Their ancient roots were being restored to them.

But the reform did not stop with ceremony. Every day, as he had done for several hours at the Water Gate, Ezra continued to read from the scroll during the Feast of Booths. And when the feast was over, just over three weeks after the original Water Gate reading, the people held a solemn assembly, "fasting and wearing sackcloth and having dust on their heads" (9:1).

Fasting in the same way that Nehemiah had done in faraway Susa, mourning in sackcloth, they gather to meet with their God. A new awareness has been born among them. Not only have they been re-awakened to a sense of their national identity and history but to a deep consciousness of Yahweh their God. They now see their history in the framework of the covenants and through the eyes of the prophets.

After several hours, "a quarter of the day," of Scripture reading they give themselves to more hours of public prayer (9:3). The formal record of the prayer is stunning in its scope and vision. Not since Solomon's prayer at the opening of the Temple has such a public prayer been uttered (9:5-38 and 2 Chron 6:12-42). The prayer leads into a binding agreement signed by Nehemiah, the priests and the Levites, and agreed to by the rest of the people who bind themselves under a curse to keep the law of Moses (10:1-29). They mention specific failures that had to be rectified immediately and commit themselves to do so (10:30-39). The nation has been born anew. The Spirit of God has intervened, bringing about renewal and a profound change of heart and vision among the Jews. They are now set on the true course of their national destiny.

Nehemiah and Ezra had not themselves brought about the change. But because they had lived as men of God and men of the Word, they had created under God a climate in which renewal and reformation could take place. And they had been privileged both to see and to lead that reformation, and largely to determine the national ethos for over four hundred years.

For Individuals or Groups

1. How would you define *spiritual renewal?*
2. What can trigger a spiritual renewal?
3. In Nehemiah 8 and 9 we see that understanding leads to revival. Is this a model for all revival? Explain your response.
4. How would you evaluate the place of understanding in current presentations of the Christian faith (to Christians and non-Christians; in churches or books, on radio or television)?
5. On pages 113-14, what are said to be results of genuine renewal?
6. Do you see such signs of renewal around you? If so, why? If not, why not?

9

The
Leader &
Endurance

13 *⁴BEFORE THIS, ELIASHIB THE PRIEST HAD BEEN PUT IN CHARGE OF THE STORE-rooms of the house of our God. He was closely associated with Tobiah, and he had ⁵provided him with a large room formerly used to store the grain offerings and incense and temple articles, and also the tithes of grain, new wine and oil prescribed for the Levites, singers and gatekeepers, as well as the contributions for the priests.*

⁶But while all this was going on, I was not in Jerusalem, for in the thirty-second year of Artaxerxes king of Babylon I had returned to the king. Some time later I asked his permission ⁷and came back to Jerusalem. Here I learned about the evil thing Eliashib had done in providing Tobiah a room in the courts of the house of God. ⁸I was greatly displeased and threw all Tobiah's household goods out of the room. ⁹I gave orders to purify the rooms, and then I put back into them the equipment of the house of God, with the grain offerings and the incense.

¹⁰I also learned that the portions assigned to the Levites had not been given to them, and that all the Levites and singers responsible for the service had gone back to their own fields. ¹¹So I rebuked the officials and asked them, "Why is the house of God neglected?" Then I called them together and stationed them at their posts.

¹²All Judah brought the tithes of grain, new wine and oil into the storerooms. *13I put Shelemiah the priest, Zadok the scribe, and a Levite named Pedaiah in charge of the storerooms and made Hanan son of Zaccur, the son of Mattaniah, their assistant, because these men were considered trustworthy. They were made responsible for distributing the supplies to their brothers.*

14Remember me for this, O my God, and do not blot out what I have so faithfully done for the house of my God and its services.

15In those days I saw men in Judah treading winepresses on the Sabbath and bringing in grain and loading it on donkeys, together with wine, grapes, figs and all other kinds of loads. And they were bringing all this into Jerusalem on the Sabbath. Therefore I warned them against selling food on that day. 16Men from Tyre who lived in Jerusalem were bringing in fish and all kinds of merchandise and selling them in Jerusalem on the Sabbath to the people of Judah. 17I rebuked the nobles of Judah and said to them, "What is this wicked thing you are doing— desecrating the Sabbath day? 18Didn't your forefathers do the same things, so that our God brought all this calamity upon us and upon this city? Now you are stirring up more wrath against Israel by desecrating the Sabbath."

19When evening shadows fell on the gates of Jerusalem before the Sabbath, I ordered the doors to be shut and not opened until the Sabbath was over. I stationed some of my own men at the gates so that no load could be brought in on the Sabbath day. 20Once or twice the merchants and sellers of all kinds of goods spent the night outside Jerusalem. 21But I warned them and said, "Why do you spend the night by the wall? If you do this again, I will lay hands on you." From that time on they no longer came on the Sabbath. 22Then I commanded the Levites to purify themselves and go and guard the gates in order to keep the Sabbath day holy.

Remember me for this also, O my God, and show mercy to me according to your great love.

23Moreover, in those days I saw men of Judah who had married women from Ashdod, Ammon and Moab. 24Half of their children spoke the language of Ashdod or the language of one of the other peoples, and

did not know how to speak the language of Judah. *25I rebuked them and
called curses down on them. I beat some of the men and pulled out their
hair. I made them take an oath in God's name and said: "You are not
to give your daughters in marriage to their sons, nor are you to take their
daughters in marriage for your sons or for yourselves. 26Was it not
because of marriages like these that Solomon king of Israel sinned?
Among the many nations there was no king like him. He was loved by
his God, and God made him king over all Israel, but even he was led
into sin by foreign women. 27Must we hear now that you too are doing
all this terrible wickedness and are being unfaithful to our God by
marrying foreign women?"*

*28One of the sons of Joiada son of Eliashib the high priest was son-
in-law to Sanballat the Horonite. And I drove him away from me.*

*29Remember them, O my God, because they defiled the priestly office
and the covenant of the priesthood and of the Levites.*

*30So I purified the priests and the Levites of everything foreign, and
assigned them duties, each to his own task. 31I also made provision for
contributions of wood at designated times, and for the firstfruits.*

Remember me with favor, O my God.

The last lap of the race can be killing. But it is also a key lap. It
can be the most challenging, the lap that "sorts out the men from
the boys," the test of those runners with "what it really takes."

The last lap of life, the lap of old age, is the lap all of us must prepare
to run one day. Mental preparation for that lap should begin at the
beginning of the race. Good runners always run a race with the last lap
in mind and have a realistic grasp of what the last lap might involve.

Physically, life's last lap can be hard. Joints creak. Strength ebbs. Hair
and teeth fall out, faces wrinkle and bodies grow distorted in appear-
ance. Memory fades and plays tricks.

Socially, psychologically and spiritually it is even more difficult. Those
in the streets treat older people either patronizingly or with brutal indifference. In stores the question, "Are you a senior citizen, ma'am?"
may be kindly intentioned, but it can be an irritating reminder that one

is no longer to be taken seriously.

To be a young Christian can mean to be applauded and encouraged in one's efforts. To be old may mean to be forgotten. I remember standing outside a nursing home and being told of an outstanding internationally known missionary who was living, lonely and forgotten, inside. Yet his last days had to be lived. In that sense he was still running. How well will I run if no one but Christ watches my last lap? From Christ's point of view, that last lap matters supremely.

It is therefore imperative that by the time we are old we have learned not to accept society's view of us. Though physical discomfort, mental weariness and lack of encouragement cause us to long for peace, we must pay no heed. There is a race to be run, and run we must for the race has to be finished.

Old age has not always been despised. The aged in most cultures and in most periods of history have not only had a place in society, but a highly respected one. Increasingly this is changing.

Some years ago I was moved by an account in *Time* magazine of a visit by Richard Nixon to the aging Nikita Khrushchev. Their first Russian encounter, televised to the world, had been the famous kitchen debate. Few people who saw it will forget Nixon's finger indignantly jabbing toward Khrushchev's barrel chest. At that time Nixon was vice president in the Eisenhower administration in the United States and Khrushchev the ruler of Russia. But now Nixon was the leader of the world's most powerful nation and Khrushchev no longer had any power. They found him forgotten and ignored, living in cramped quarters in a small apartment. Once the ruler of the world's second most powerful nation, Nikita Khrushchev had become a forgotten nobody. The old wolf had been driven from the pack.

The twentieth century has seen other elderly statesmen function superbly in old age. Charles De Gaulle, Konrad Adenauer, Deng Xiaoping and Ronald Reagan exemplify the possibility of retaining power and pre-eminence. But it is one thing for a leader to cling to power in the face of competition and opposition, and another to run the last lap of life well. After all, some leaders die in power, propped up by the system to the last. We are not talking about coming in first but about running magnificently. Heaven's awards are not based on the same criteria as those of politics and competitive sports.

What happens to Christian leaders in old age? How well do the Christian stars run when the specter of age runs beside them? How many of them continue to run hard? Do they focus on retaining their youthful image? (Denial of failing powers is futile. We have to face them and focus on using what powers we retain.) Do they become cranky and bigoted? Seek ease and grow self-indulgent? Start to live in the past?

Nehemiah's age remains a secret to the end of the book. Perhaps he wasn't what we might call old. What, after all, is *old?* But certainly in chapter 13 he was old*er.* His first period in Jerusalem lasted twelve years (5:14). Following this he returned to Susa for an unknown number of years before coming back for a second term as governor (13:6-7). The incidents that he describes in the thirteenth chapter belong to this period.

If he had been forty years old when he first arrived in Jerusalem (and he could have been seven or eight years older or younger), then he would have returned to Susa at the age of fifty-two. How many years passed before he returned to Jerusalem? All we can say is that during his second period he was "not as young as he used to be." And reactions described in the chapter have about them more than a trace of the kind of irascibility that is associated with age. Indeed some people would say he had become irascible, violent and autocratic.

Like the first seven chapters, the last chapter of the book was written by Nehemiah in the first person singular. It is here that we are able to look at a leader in later life. It is here too that his toughness becomes most apparent. If throughout his earlier career he is seen as decisive and active, he is more so than ever in this phase of his leadership. Consider some of the verbs in chapter 13: "I . . . threw . . . out [v. 8] . . . I gave orders [v. 9] . . . I rebuked [v. 11] . . . I called them together [v. 11] . . . I put . . . in charge [v. 13] . . . I warned [v. 15] . . . I ordered [v. 19] . . . I stationed [v. 19] . . . I warned [v. 21] . . . I commanded [v. 22] . . . I rebuked . . . called curses . . . beat . . . pulled out their hair. I made them take an oath [v. 25] . . . I drove . . . away [v. 28] . . . I purified [v. 30]."

On his return to Jerusalem he finds that the reformation movement that began so well is no longer going forward. The solemn vows of the past have evidently been forgotten. Tobiah's influence over the high priest has led to flagrant desecration of the Temple (13:4-5). Temple worship has also deteriorated as funds to support Levites and singers have dried up (13:10). Commerce has undermined Sabbath observance (13:15) and mixed marriages now pose a threat to Hebrew culture (13:23). Let us consider each of these four problems in turn.

The Courage to Act

Godly leaders, as we have seen, do not only face opposition from outside the ranks of the faithful but also from within. The most painful hurts to Christians leaders come from those who call themselves Christians. "Even my close friend, whom I trusted, he who shared my bread, has lifted up his heel against me," cries David in deep distress (Ps 41:9). And Jesus echoes his words (Jn 13:18). His love for Judas had been open and genuine. Treachery from within wounds more deeply than arrows fired by an enemy.

It was for this reason that Nehemiah's concern about the abuse of the Temple was more focused on Eliashib the high priest than with Tobiah the Ammonite. Tobiah had been a thorn in Nehemiah's side for long enough. With Sanballat he had taunted Nehemiah and plotted his downfall (2:10, 19; 4:3, 7; 6:1, 14). But as Nehemiah's star continued to rise, Tobiah's strategy changed subtly (6:17-19). Increasingly he sought to ingratiate himself with whomever was important and influential in Jerusalem.

In the process he may have been trying to become Jewish. To some scholars his very name suggests this. But if so, he faced an extreme difficulty. He belonged to a race whose members would never be welcome in "the assembly of God" (Neh 13:1; Deut 23:3-4). Nevertheless, by a strategic series of marriage alliances he had moved into a powerful position in Jerusalem (6:18; 13:4).

And it is here that another difficulty arises for godly leaders. Ties of blood and of marriage can make difficult disciplinary decisions even more difficult.

Nehemiah had for years shown himself capable of coping with Tobiah. And even though Tobiah's influence over the high priest was great enough for the high priest to clear out a large and important room in the Temple, turning it into a private apartment for Tobiah (13:4-7), it was Eliashib's action that would embarrass Nehemiah the most. "Here I learned about the evil thing Eliashib had done in providing Tobiah a room in the courts of the house of God" (13:7). Nehemiah would have to take an unpleasant action Eliashib was too weak to take.

Nehemiah's action is violent. He throws Tobiah's possessions out and, more significantly, orders a ritual cleansing of the rooms he has occupied (13:8-9). Though his action may seem to be directed against his old enemy, it is only incidentally so. For how will Eliashib react?

Eliashib is in charge of the Temple. He was "put in charge of the storerooms of the house of . . . God" (13:4). There has always been a tension between civil and religious authorities. And one can imagine a stronger priest than Eliashib saying to Nehemiah, "I can understand your hostility to Tobiah, but you have no right to barge in here and particularly no right to order a ritual cleansing of rooms that I, who am in charge, had assigned to Tobiah. Any ritual cleansing around here takes place at *my* orders. This is *my* territory."

We are not told what Eliashib's reaction was. But Nehemiah would be aware of the political nature of his action. It might be a setback for Tobiah. But to the high priest it would be an open humiliation and rebuke.

Nehemiah's violent reaction in a way anticipates Christ's own Temple cleansing. It is not only violent but seems autocratic. Nehemiah was upset and he knew it. He was "greatly displeased." But does his distress over a genuine wrong, even a wrong which had desecrated the Temple, justify such an approach? Could the matter have been handled more diplomatically? More judiciously?

Doubtless we could debate the subject. Yet in Christian work our cowardice in avoiding unpleasantness is currently doing more damage than any damage from irascibility on the part of Christian leaders. And what irascibility we do give way to is usually verbal. It wounds without correcting. The church has become flabby, old womanish, inept, unwilling to *act*. Discipline should be reconciliatory and loving, *but it should take place*. And on the whole it doesn't.

Nehemiah in old age is to be commended for his courage, his firmness, his willingness to face issues and to do something about them. Even the way he acts is justifiable once we understand both Mosaic law and the cultural context. Who are we—who condone every manner of evil in our midst—to criticize one of those rare leaders who does not hesitate to act when the integrity of God's Temple is in question?

Unpopular Priorities

To the end of his life Nehemiah remained a leader who could and did take an unpopular course when he saw it to be necessary. This brings us to the second issue requiring his attention: the deterioration of Temple worship. The very room that had been allocated to Tobiah was the room where "income" for the Levites and singers was stored. The tithe to support them and to enable them to carry out their ritual functions was given mainly in the form of grain, oil and wine. It is likely that the public protest against Tobiah's occupation of those particular chambers would be muted. Few people would be enthusiastic about paying tithes. And if there was nowhere to store the tithe, it would be less likely than ever that tithes would be collected properly. Conscientious tithers might feel uneasy, might even be critical of the situation. But they would not be likely to insist that matters be rectified. Taxes had to be paid. But tithes were a religious matter and burdensome to a subject people struggling for economic recovery.

The only folk who might feel strongly would be people whose salaries were affected by unpaid tithes. These included the Levites (who were responsible for many practical matters connected with the Temple worship), the priests (a Levitical clan responsible for offering sacrifices and prayers on behalf of the people), and the musicians and singers (whose services were part of ongoing Temple worship).

No doubt Eliashib's personal financial needs would be cared for. Sacrifices would still be offered. But many Levites and singers would go hungry. "The portions assigned to the Levites had not been given to them, and . . . all the Levites and singers responsible for the service had gone back to their own fields" (13:10). The time they should have been spending on their Temple duties was spent on cultivating fields to feed themselves.

One outstanding aspect of the re-establishment of the nation concerned its priorities. From the outset God had come first. First, the altar was built that sacrifices might be offered (Ezra 3:3). Then, before any attempt was made to rebuild Jerusalem's walls, the Temple was rebuilt, the Passover celebrated with generous abandon, and priest and Levites appointed (Ezra 6:15-18). The Jews were not just any people. They were people chosen by God, delivered from bondage and entrusted with God's laws.

But priorities slip with the passage of time, especially where those priorities touch our pocketbook. Once Nehemiah grasps the situation, he acts. He reprimands those at fault (13:11), restarts the practice of tithing (13:12) and appoints reliable officers to supervise its administration (13:13).

His action is remarkable when we consider that he stood to gain nothing personally from what he did. We are accustomed to financial appeals from executives and leaders supervising the work for which the appeal is being made. The church treasurer and the chairperson of the building committee will appeal for funds for the projected education wing. The pastor might also boost the appeal. But it would be surprising to find a local politician intervening and making sure that the thing was carried through.

In a sense that was what happened here. If anybody should have been interested enough to act, it should have been Eliashib. The Temple was his responsibility. Its proper running would be to his credit. Nehemiah stood to gain nothing personally by reproving greed and selfishness and re-establishing an adequate financial basis for proper Temple worship.

Nehemiah's priorities were God's priorities. At a time when it would be easy to be discouraged, to sit back and let matters slip, he took precise and effective action to restore what was lacking. His leadership reveals, as it had from the first, a policy of putting first things first. He accepted God's priorities whether they might be popular or unpopular, whether they would be to his personal advantage or not.

Where money is concerned we need leaders of this sort. The Christian system in the West is basically need-oriented. Organizers perceive a need and make an appeal to the Christian public on that basis. The most effective appeals are based more on mass psychology than on godliness and often have little relevance to the real nature of Christ's kingdom. Yet Christ's priorities are not buildings and prestige but people, oppressed and disadvantaged people in physical, emotional and spiritual bondage.

The problem is complex and multifaceted. I have tried to deal with the principles in *The Golden Cow*. The church needs to be instructed in giving as *worship* and as *true fellowship with the distressed*. We need prophets who will perceive finance as God perceives it and responsible leaders who will act according to those principles. In the process they will serve God but they are not likely to become popular.

Business and Rest

Mammon is a powerful and relentless pursuer of our worship. He was as active among Jerusalem Jews as he is in the twentieth century. He was the source of Nehemiah's third area of concern on returning to Jerusalem. And Nehemiah is again quick to act.

The Sabbath was desecrated by commerce (13:15-18). The wine presses continued to be trod and donkeys to be loaded every day of the week. The produce of the fields was also brought into Jerusalem markets on the Sabbath. Merchants came even from Tyre with fish to sell.

Nehemiah is practical. Long ago he had seen to it that stout gates were hung in Jerusalem's gateways. Now he orders that the gates be closed from the evening before the Sabbath until the morning after. To make sure the orders are obeyed, he stations his servants at the gates (13:19). But traders continued to congregate outside the gates on the Sabbath and to pass the night outside with their wares, waiting for the gates to open (13:20). The practice could rapidly undermine his attempts to stop Sabbath commerce. So Nehemiah takes further steps. He personally confronts the traders. "I warned them and said, 'Why do you spend the night by the wall? If you do this again, I will lay hands on you' " (13:21). And in keeping with his threats he purifies certain Levites to become a permanent body of gatekeepers and to act as guardians of the Sabbath (13:22).

At this point he is seen supremely as the man of action. But while this aspect of his character is important in leadership, it would be wrong to suggest that the only godly leadership that counts is the leadership of godly activists. There is no evidence to suggest, for instance, that Ezra was an activist. Yet Ezra's contribution to the monumental changes that took place among the Jews is probably as great as that of Nehemiah.

No, the point I am making is that to the end of his days Nehemiah retained the same zeal that mobilized the Jews to rebuild the walls and that made him intervene earlier to abolish exploitation of the poor. Nehemiah was not a flash-in-the-pan leader but one who remained, as long as he lived, consistent to his original vision.

We might ask, of course, what bearing his actions have on the matter of Sabbath observance today. As in Christ's own day, people are inclined to perceive only the letter of the law and fail to understand the principle.

Christ laid the basis for our understanding when he pointed out that the Sabbath was made to benefit human beings (Mk 2:27). As for the commercial activity Nehemiah squelched, we see in it an example of human greed robbing people of proper rest and true recreation. One day is set aside to enable us to renew our strength and to refresh our spirits. The moment we turn that day into a legalistic test of orthodoxy, we have misunderstood its real purpose. And the moment we neglect it to make money, we damage ourselves and others and laugh at the grace of God.

Nehemiah was concerned for people. He was concerned particularly for those condemned to tread wine presses and load donkeys to make more money for their employers. True, they themselves will be paid wages. But employees and employers alike have to be taught that man does not live by bread alone.

Meddling with Marriages

The problem with God is that he tells people how to live. And people don't like to be told. Christian leaders who truly teach may find themselves instructing God's people about touchy issues, touchy because feelings run deep over them. They include marital and family issues, child rearing, sexual morality and suicide, the most elemental aspects of our humanity.

In societies whose values are in conflict with biblical values, Christians will find themselves increasingly facing opposition and even litigation merely for teaching something biblical. The pastor who tells someone that his understanding of Scripture does not lead him to believe that Christians will lose their salvation if they commit suicide may be sued by the parents of a young Christian who subsequently does. Churches exercising discipline in sexual matters are being sued for invasion of privacy. Western secular society in its ever-increasing devotion to what it considers individual rights, shows increasing signs of resenting church authority in church matters. Courage and wisdom will be needed in Christian leadership.

Marriage is a particularly difficult area in which to exert strong leadership. Nehemiah, in responding to this fourth and final problem area, would have encountered profound resentment as he attempts to regulate Jewish marriages. Jewish men had not only married outside the faith, but had chosen brides from among the especially forbidden nations (13:23). Ezra had faced a similar problem years before (Ezra 9:1-2). He had gone much further than Nehemiah, calling upon men to put away foreign wives on pain of their being excluded from the commonwealth of Israel (Ezra 9:11).

The account of what happened in Ezra is painful. Hundreds of families are involved. A large assembly of people meets weeping before a weeping Ezra. Clearly Ezra himself is no shallow legalist but a man appalled by what he sees as a horrendous situation (Ezra 9:3-4). Indeed he perceives the guilt of the people as his own guilt (Ezra 9:5-15).

Perhaps because of Ezra's radical stand, Nehemiah's task is easier. At any rate he does not insist on the stronger position taken by Ezra. His account may help us to grasp what had been at stake. In both cases disobedience to the law threatened the very existence of the Jewish identity. Nehemiah became aware that half of the children of mixed marriages "spoke the language of Ashdod . . . *and did not know how to speak the language of Judah*" (13:24).

Culture, religion, national identity—all depend on language. Children who do not speak the language of their fathers are cut off from their fathers' heritage. Children who speak only the language of their mothers are exposed predominantly to the culture, the values, the history, traditions and lifestyle of their mothers. At the very point in history at which a nation is being re-established, mixed marriages threaten to obliterate all that makes that nation distinctive. It could easily have become another nation entirely, beginning as a multiethnic group, a cultural mosaic, to merge into a new race with traditions blended of everything that God called Abram out from. And language was a key factor.

Certainly this was clear to Nehemiah. And if his action is less traumatic than Ezra's, it is vigorous enough. He contends with the offenders, curses them, strikes some of them and pulls out their hair. He makes parents swear not to negotiate mixed marriages for their children. And he gives them a thorough verbal drubbing (13:25-27).

It is not the kind of approach we would welcome in Christian churches where irregularities have to be dealt with. Nor should it be. It reflects the culture where shame is a powerful weapon for social cohesion. Nehemiah publicly shames the wrongdoers. His diatribe both shames and instructs wrongdoers and potential wrongdoers alike.

In this case a desperate ill has called for desperate remedies and Nehemiah, like Ezra before him, is willing to administer the medicine full strength. Even though issues of this sort can be highly controversial, he does not sidestep his responsibility to deal with them.

We are not being given here a model for Christian marriage in general. While we are told to eschew marrying out of the faith (2 Cor 6:14), once the marriage is in existence we are nowhere encouraged to break it. The Christian partner is, on the contrary, instructed to act as a Christian within the marriage.

No, the lesson for us here is a lesson in leadership. Once again we are called to see an older leader, faithful to the end, clinging to values he knows to be God's values despite their likely unpopularity.

Pathos in Prayer

The book of Nehemiah opens in prayer and closes in prayer. Nowhere do we perceive Nehemiah's heart more clearly than in his prayers. And yet his briefer prayers, scattered throughout his journal, may puzzle and even disappoint us. They lack high-minded, high-arching altruistic spirituality and poetic insight. They do not seem woven of the same cloth as the prayers admired by people who appreciate fine sentiments and good literature. They are crude, pain-soaked cries.

Earlier I suggested that part of the reason they disappoint us may lie in our own dishonesty. Nehemiah's prayers, unlike David's (though there are some problems with David's too), are not polished compositions so much as cries of primitive pain from a lonely man. And sometimes we, anxious to pray "proper" and "spiritual" prayers, do not dare to look into the depths of our sinful hearts. Our discomfort with Nehemiah arises because Nehemiah does what we would all like to do—to express what we really feel.

What, after all, does he ask for in the last four prayers he records (13:14, 22, 29, 31)? He asks that God *remember*. The word sets the tone in all four prayers. Does he feel that God will be forgetful? Or is it that, like us, he is so painfully aware of his smallness and of the manifold and overarching concerns of the great God he addresses that he fears his life is too unimportant for God to keep him constantly in mind? His problem is not primarily with God's character but with his own importance.

So we object because his prayers draw attention to his good works. "Remember me for this, O my God, and do not blot out what I have so faithfully done for the house of my God and its services" (13:14). Does he base his hopes on his own righteousness, on his own works? It seems unlikely when we think of his prayer in chapter 1. At even this point in his life he pleads God's compassion not on the basis of his works but "according to your great love" (13:22).

Surely to mention one's good works to God is not in itself wrong. It is not necessarily to pray like the Pharisee in the Temple (Lk 18:10-14). Nehemiah longed for reassurance. Is it wrong for children to want their father to see what they have done? Wrong to want praise, not from people, but from God? And if Nehemiah wants the evil deeds of others to be remembered too (13:29), surely we can see that an assurance that God is a God of justice must precede a comprehension of him as a God of mercy. Mercy that springs from injustice is not mercy but compromise.

So what do Nehemiah's prayers tell us of the aging Nehemiah? They reveal to us the heart of a man continually under pressure in the lonely struggle against evil. They also reflect a man who walks in a moment-by-moment awareness of God. Finally they reflect a man for whom the highest accolade is, as Derek Kidner points out (*Ezra & Nehemiah,* IVP), God's smile of approval, an attitude which is surely an effective defense against spiritual pride.

Nehemiah was human. We need not speculate on his weaknesses for we have our own. Rather we must be grateful for what we have learned from him. The fact that he was shaped from ordinary clay to become the leader he was should surely encourage us.

He has shown us the worthwhileness of waiting on God in prayer and that all real planning begins in God's presence. His example has made it clear that true leadership must be consistent with an ongoing servanthood. We have seen that his concern for God's priorities and for the people of Jerusalem determined his leadership style. He taught us the value of keeping ultimate goals always in mind and rebuked us with his attitude to money. We have watched him move from stress to stress and from strength to strength as he walks through the doors of fear to ultimate triumph.

And finally we have seen that he continued to run as well in the closing laps of the race as he had in the opening. The same faith and obedience that led him to take huge risks in the presence of King Artaxerxes continued to motivate him toward the close of his life.

It is time now for us to bid him farewell. We may not play so important a role in history as he. But we can run as well as he did. It is imperative that we, like Paul in 2 Timothy 4:7, be able to say one day, "I have fought the good fight, *I have finished the race.*"

For Individuals or Groups

1. What do you see as the greatest obstacles to persevering to old age as a Christian? Explain.
2. For what unpleasant tasks do you need the courage to act? How can you get that courage?
3. How can we, like Nehemiah, help people recapture a biblical view of giving?
4. How has the purpose of the Sabbath been diluted in our society, in the church and in your own life? How can the imbalance be corrected?
5. Why is it so difficult to help people follow the lifestyle God lays out in Scripture? Have there been times in your life when you resented God telling you how to live? Explain.
6. What do you want God to remember about you in your old age? Why?

The Fight

JOHN WHITE

John White has written this book because he wants you to understand clearly what the Christian life is all about. He wants you to learn in the depths of your being that the eternal God loves you and plans only your highest good – more trust in him, more likeness to him.

But his love will bring pain as intense as your joy. For the Christian life is a fight....

"Reading *The Fight* is to inhale great draughts of fresh air into one's Christian life... This is the kind of book every 20th Century Christian should have on his book shelf."

Christian Weekly Newspapers

230 pages   Pocketbook

Inter-Varsity Press

Eros Defiled

JOHN WHITE

To be human is to be sexual. That's the way God made us.

Yet many people – Christians included – are tormented by their sexuality. The problem may be frustration, masturbation, premarital sex and perhaps pregnancy, an 'affair', homosexuality, or strange compulsions.

To these people and their counsellors, John White offers compassion, help and hope.

"… a refreshing direct book. It.. shows a great deal of sensitivity, and has no fear of straight speaking."   Christian Weekly Newspapers

"The book's arguments are carefully anchored in the Bible. Undoubtedly *Eros Defiled* should be required reading for all in the pastoral ministry… Youth leaders… parents too. It can be recommended also to Christian adolescents in their late teens."   Evangelical Times

168 pages   Pocketbook

Inter-Varsity Press

The Cost of Commitment

JOHN WHITE

'For years I felt guilty because I never seemed to be committed deeply enough to Christ... I had the feeling that I should be suffering more, doing without more. Yet when I did suffer, my suffering bore little relationship to my commitment. Sometimes it seemed to arise from my lack of commitment and at other times bore no relation at all to it...

'When Jesus tells you to take up your cross daily, he is not telling you to find some way to suffering daily. He is simply giving forewarning of what happens to the person who follows him.'

A warm and personal book to help Christians count the cost of commitment.

"...message is presented in a lucid, readable, at times very moving style.."   Evangelical Times

".. useful book to place into the hands of those who have recently made the great decision."
Christian Herald

91 pages   Pocketbook

Inter-Varsity Press